Putnam's Concise

MYTHOLOGICAL
DICTIONARY

D1383972

Putnam's Concise

MYTHOLOGICAL DICTIONARY

by Joseph Kaster

BASED UPON *GODS*
BY BESSIE REDFIELD

A PERIGEE BOOK

NOTE: A book entitled *Gods, A Dictionary of the Deities of All Lands*, compiled and edited by Bessie G. Redfield, was issued by the same publishers in 1931. The present work is a complete and thorough revision of that book, for the purpose of producing a concise and accurate dictionary founded upon scholarly research. Only part of the title and the structural format have been retained. Otherwise it is a completely new book.

© 1963 by G. P. Putnam's Sons
Copyright 1931 by Bessie Gordon Redfield
Perigee Books
are published by
G. P. Putnam's Sons
200 Madison Avenue
New York, New York, 10016

Library of Congress Catalog Card Number: 63-9663

SBN: 399-50050-2
First Perigee Printing, 1980

MANUFACTURED IN THE UNITED STATES OF AMERICA

FOREWORD

This dictionary is intended to serve as a ready and convenient reference aid for the general reader, for quick and handy elucidation of the nature of a deity or a mythological term which he would ordinarily encounter in general literature.

Many of the deities and their myths have, over the centuries, been interpreted and reinterpreted to suit the whims and personal bias of generations of writers, with the result that a host of romantic, mystic or religious misinterpretations, egregious errors, and traditional expurgations have been perpetuated from one popular dictionary to another. This dictionary, while popular, is based upon works of genuine scholarship which embody the results of scientific research, a few of which are mentioned in the bibliography. It is hoped that this little book, while serving as a useful tool, will stimulate the reader's curiosity to explore some of these works. He will be well rewarded.

J. K.

FOR FURTHER
REFERENCE

The literature on mythology, scholarly and otherwise, is immense. The following selected list has been confined to works which have been written by serious and scientific scholars and are available in English. Most of these works are relatively inexpensive and easily obtainable.

Rose, H. J., *Gods and Heroes of the Greeks*. New York: Meridian Books.

Guthrie, W. K. C., *The Greeks and Their Gods*. Boston: Beacon Press.

Seyffert, Oskar, *Dictionary of Classical Antiquities*. Rev. ed., Nettleship and Sandys. New York: Meridian Books.

Cerny, Jaroslav, *Ancient Egyptian Religion*. Hutchinson's University Library.

Hooke, S. H., *Babylonian and Assyrian Religion*. Hutchinson's University Library.

Sjoestedt, Marie-Louise, *Gods and Heroes of the Celts*. Translated by Myles Dillon. London: Methuen.

Gordon, Cyrus H., "Canaanite Mythology," *Mythologies of the Ancient World*, ed. S. N. Kramer. New York: Doubleday-Anchor.

Sykes, Egerton (ed.), *Everyman's Dictionary of Non-Classical Mythology*. New York: Everyman's Library, Dutton.

A few larger works for consultation by those interested in further study:

The Oxford Classical Dictionary. Oxford University Press.

Jacobus, Lane and Zenos (eds.), *A New Standard Bible Dictionary*. Third rev. ed., New York: Funk and Wagnalls.

Interpreter's Dictionary of the Bible. 4 vols. Abingdon Press.

Standard Dictionary of Folklore, Mythology and Legend. 2 vols. New York: Funk and Wagnalls.

Terms printed in SMALL CAPITALS within a definition will also be found as separate entries in the dictionary. The reader is advised to consult these for further elucidation.

A

Aaru, Aalu: see YAARU

Abaddon: in Hebrew, *lit.* "the place of the lost," or "perdition," used in medieval myth as a synonym for Hell and/or the ruler thereof.

Abaris: a priest of APOLLO, who, with the help of the god, fled from Scythia (in the Caucasus) to Greece to avoid a plague. Apollo gave him a miraculous golden arrow which rendered him invisible, and with which he cured diseases and gave oracles.

Abracadabra: a medieval spell or charm serving as a TALISMAN against diseases and other perils. The term may be derived from the Aramaic *avada kedavra,* "may the thing be destroyed."

Abundantia: minor Roman goddess, a personification of abundance and plenty.

Acheloüs: ancient Greek river-deity, eldest son of OCEANUS and TETHYS. Assuming the form of a bull, he fought with HERACLES for DEIANIRA, but was vanquished by Heracles, who broke off one of his horns, which, according to one tradition, became the *Cornucopia,* or "horn of plenty."

Acheron: the name of several rivers believed to flow through the realms of HADES, and by poetical metaphor, often Hades itself.

Achilles: son of PELEUS and THETIS, and hero of the *Iliad.* While he was an infant, his mother sought to make him immortal by dipping him in the river STYX, but since she held him by the heel, that part proved to be vulnerable to death. Thetis also told him that he had the choice of either a life long but uneventful, or one short but glorious, and he chose the latter. He assumed a most important role in the Achaean war with Troy, and his feud with AGAMEMNON and its resolution forms the central theme of the *Iliad*. He was killed, in the last days of the siege of Troy, by an arrow wound in his heel.

Acis: legendary Sicilian shepherd, son of FAUNUS and a nymph. He was beloved of the nymph GALATEA, but was slain by his rival, the CYCLOPS POLYPHEMUS.

Acrisius: King of Argos and father of DANAË.

Actaeon: legendary Greek huntsman, son of Aristaeus and AUTONOË, daughter of CADMUS. He was turned into a stag by ARTEMIS and torn to pieces by his hounds, either because he came upon the naked goddess while she was bathing, or because he boasted of excelling her in hunting.

Adapa: in ancient Sumero-Akkadian myth, the first man created by EA (ENKI), and king and priest of the ancient Sumerian city of Eridu. He broke the wing of the south wind when it overturned his fishing-boat and so had to appear before ANU. Adapa's father Ea had instructed him to refuse the bread and water of death which Anu would offer him, but Anu offered him the bread and water of life which Adapa, obedient to instructions, refused. Thus he had to remain mortal, and disease and death became the lot of mankind.

Aditya, Adityas: in Hindu myth, the primeval mother-goddess, embodiment of the generative forces of nature, and progenitress of all things DAKSHA is mentioned as both her son and her father, and VISHNU as both consort and son. She is the mother of the *Adityas,* the gods of the months of the year: ANSA, ARYMAN, BHAGA, DAKSHA, DHATRI, INDRA, MITRA, RAVI, SAVITRI, SURYA, VARUNA and YAMA.

Adonai (see also ADONIS): Hebrew word meaning "my lord, my master," from *adon,* "lord, master." From Hellenistic times onward it was used verbally to replace the written YAHWEH.

Adonis: in Greek myth, the youth beloved by APHRODITE. He died of a wound inflicted by a boar in the hunt, and the inconsolable Aphrodite made the Anemone grow from his blood. In Hades PERSEPHONE fell in love with him, but in pity for the great grief of Aphrodite, ZEUS decreed that Adonis was to spend six months of the year in the underworld and the other six with Aphrodite in the upper. The myth and ritual of Adonis, with the weeping for the slain youth and joy at his resurrection, was imported from Syria, where he was identified with TAMMUZ. His name is also Syrian, from the Semitic *Adon,* "lord, master," and has the same meaning as BAAL.

Adrasteia (Adrastea): "she whom none can escape," properly an epithet of RHEA CYBELE in her attribute of the Mother who punishes human injustice, which is a transgression of the natural right order of things. She was identified by the Greeks and Romans with NEMESIS.

Aeacus: son of ZEUS and AEGINA, daughter of the river-god ASOPUS. ZEUS carried her off to an island off Attica, which was called *Aegina* after her. Aeacus reigned afterwards in Aegina, and was so renowned for his piety that after his death he was made one of the judges of the realms of HADES.

Aeëtes: son of HELIOS and an OCEANID, and brother of CIRCE and PASIPHAË. He was king of Colchis, and when PHRIXUS came to his court he killed him in order to obtain the golden fleece of the ram upon which Phrixus had fled. Aeëtes then had the fleece guarded by fire-breathing bulls and a venomous dragon. When the ARGONAUTS came to Colchis, under the leadership of JASON, to fetch the golden fleece, they were aided by MEDEA, the daughter of Aeëtes.

Aegaeon: an Homeric epithet for BRIAREUS. He is also represented as a son of POSEIDON, and a marine deity of the Aegaean Sea.

Aegaeus: legendary king of early Athens and father of THESEUS. He had been driven from the throne, but was restored to it by Theseus when the latter came to Athens after his youthful adventures. Theseus, when he sailed to Crete to deliver Athens from the Minoan tribute, had promised his father that if the mission were successful he would hoist white sails on his ship on the return voyage, replacing the mournful black ones with which it had set out. He forgot to do so, and Aegaeus, seeing the black sails and thinking that his son had perished, threw himself into the sea, whence it received its name, *Aegaean*.

Aegina: daughter of the river-god ASOPUS, from whom ZEUS carried her off to an island in the Saronic Gulf off Attica. The island was named *Aegina* after her. She became by Zeus the mother of AEACUS.

Aegir: Norse god of the sea, regarded as a giant whose wild nature had to be kept in subjection by the great gods. His consort was RAN, and they had nine daughters who are described as waves of the sea.

Aegis: the awesome protective device associated with ZEUS and ATHENA. It is variously considered to be the bright-edged thundercloud, fashioned by HEPHAESTUS, or the skin of the divine goat AMALTHEIA who had nourished the infant Zeus. In any case it is normally represented as a sort of skin, sometimes covered with scales and fringed about with serpents. In the middle of the aegis is the head of MEDUSA the GORGON.

Aegisthus: son of THYESTES (according to one tradition by his own daughter Pelopia), nephew of ATREUS and hence cousin to AGAMEMNON, king of Mycenae. Taking advantage of Agamemnon's absence during the Trojan War, he became the paramour of the latter's wife CLYTEMNESTRA and usurped the throne. He and Clytemnestra murdered Agamemnon on his return from Troy, but they were soon after slain by Agamemnon's son ORESTES in revenge.

Aegle: one of the HESPERIDES.

Aegyptus: king of Egypt, son of BELUS and twin brother of DANAÜS. His fifty sons pursued the DANAÏDES to Argos, forced them to become their wives, and were slain on their wedding night by the Danaïdes, with the exception of LYNCEUS, who was spared by HYPERMNESTRA.

Aëllo: one of the three HARPIES.

Aeneas: one of the Trojan leaders in the Homeric epics, and the hero of the *Aeneid,* the later Roman epic written (in Latin) by Vergil in imitation of the Homeric poems. He was the son of APHRODITE and ANCHISES. In the *Aeneid,* Aeneas escapes from burning Troy, where his wife had perished, carrying his old father Anchises on his shoulders, and leading his little son by the hand. He goes through various perils and adventures, and finally arrives at Latium in Italy, becoming the ancestral father of the Roman people, and particularly of the house of Caesar.

Aeolus: according to some traditions, a son of POSEIDON and ruler of the Aeolian island. He was given dominion over the winds, which he kept in vast caves. He gave ODYSSEUS a bag of winds to help him on his voyage homeward, but Odysseus's men opened the bag and the winds escaped.

Aesculapius (Asclepius, Greek Asklepios): legendary Greek physician, later deified as god of the healing arts and son of APOLLO and CORONIS. He was able not only to heal the sick, but to bring back the dead to life, and therefore ZEUS destroyed him with a thunderbolt lest men learn to evade death. Those who visited his temple in Epidaurus, in Greece, would sleep there in order to receive, in their dreams, the means of recovering their health. Serpents and cocks were sacred to him.

Aesir: in Norse myth, the gods who form the entourage of ODIN and dwell in ASGARD. Their number is sometimes given as twelve, although many more are included.

Aeson: father of JASON, and rightful king of Iolcus in Thessaly. He was kept from the throne by his half brother PELIAS, who sent Jason on the expedition of the ARGONAUTS to fetch the golden fleece. According to one version, on the return of the Argonauts Aeson's youth was restored to him by the sorcery of MEDEA.

Aether: personification of "etherial" space in the early Greek cosmogonies, son of EREBUS (Darkness) and his sister NOX (Night) and brother of HEMERA (Day). In the Orphic mystical theology, Aether is the soul of the world, from which all life emanates.

Agamemnon: son of ATREUS and brother of MENE-LAOS. He married CLYTEMNESTRA, daughter of Tyndareus, king of Sparta. Agamemnon later became king of Mycenae, and organized the expedition of the Achaeans against Troy at the behest of Menelaos in consequence of the latter's wife HELEN's abduction by PARIS. When the Achaean fleet was delayed at Aulis by unfavorable winds, Agamemnon was commanded by Calchas, priest and prophet of APOLLO, to sacrifice his daughter IPHIGENIA to ARTEMIS, upon which the winds became favorable once more. Upon his return home from Troy, he was murdered by his wife, Clytemnestra, and her paramour AEGISTHUS, who, with the connivance of Clytemnestra, had usurped his throne during his absence.

Agavë: daughter of CADMUS, king of Thebes, and sister of INO and SEMELE, and mother of PENTHEUS. Pentheus, after he had become king, resisted the introduction of the worship of DIONYSUS, with the consequence that Agavë was driven into a mad Bacchic frenzy, and with the MAENADS tore her son to pieces.

Aglaia: "the brilliant, shining one," the youngest of the three GRACES, or CHARITES, and sometimes represented as wife of HEPHAESTUS.

Agni: in Hindu myth, god of the divine fire and the spirit of the SOMA. He forms one of the divine triads, with INDRA and SURYA.

Ahi: in Hindu myth, one of the forms of the serpent-god, also identified with VRITRA, whom INDRA slew with his thunderbolt, releasing the fructifying waters which Ahi withheld and was guarding.

Ahriman: in the ancient Persian (Zoroastrian) dualistic theology, the personified principle of darkness and evil, who with his cohorts is in conflict with AHURA-MAZDA, the god of light and the powers of good. At the end of the world Ahriman and his demons will be defeated.

Ahsonnutli: among the Navaho Indians, the creator of heaven and earth. He is regarded as a bisexual deity and called "the Turquoise Hermaphrodite."

Ahura-Mazda: in the ancient Persian (Zoroastrian) dualistic theology, the personified principle of light and the powers of good, the supreme beneficent deity who struggles with the equally powerful AHRIMAN, the personified principle of darkness and the powers of evil. At the end of the world Ahura-Mazda and his powers will prevail.

Aias: Greek form of the name of the Homeric hero, better known under his Latin name of AJAX, which see.

Aion: *lit.* "an age, a long space of time"; among the mystery cults of late Classical times extended to mean "everlasting, boundless time" and personified as a supreme deity and equated with ZERVAN in the association of the mysteries of ORPHEUS with those of MITHRA.

Aizen Myo-O: a Japanese god of love.

Ajax: more commonly known Latin form of the Greek AIAS. There were two heroes of this name in the Homeric epics: (1) Ajax the Greater, son of

Telamon and king of Salamis, second only to ACHILLES in bravery and strength, but far inferior in wisdom. When defeated by ODYSSEUS in the contest for the armor of Achilles, he went mad with vexation and killed himself. (2) The Lesser Ajax, prince of the Locrians, drowned after the fall of Troy either because he defied POSEIDON, or because he violated CASSANDRA in the temple of ATHENA, who caused his death.

Alaghom Naom: Mayan mother-goddess, especially associated with creation of mind and thought, known as "Mother of Mind."

Alastor: in Greek myth, an avenging demon, who visits the sins of the fathers on their children.

Albiorix: "king of the world," a tribal god of the ancient Gauls.

Alcmene: wife of AMPHITRYON of Thebes. While her husband was away fighting, ZEUS visited her in Amphitryon's guise, and she became by him the mother of HERACLES.

Alcyone: one of the PLEIADES, and beloved of POSEIDON. See also HALCYONE.

Alecto: one of the three FURIES.

Alfar: in Norse myth, a group of dwarfs or minor spirits (*elves*).

Alfheim: in Norse myth, the home of the ALFAR, the elves or dwarfs, ruled over by FREY.

Aliyn Baal, Aleyan Baal: see BAAL.

Allah: *lit.* "the god" in Arabic and the designation of the exclusively monotheistic deity in Islam.

Allat: the ancient mother and fertility goddess of the

pre-Islamic Arabs. The name means "the God-dess."

Allatu: Semitic form of the name of the Sumero-Babylonian goddess ERESHKIGAL.

Aloidae: the two mythical giants, OTUS and EPHIAL-TES, sons of POSEIDON and Canace, wife of Aloeus, who was himself Poseidon's son. Otus and Ephial-tes were renowned for their strength and daring, and in their childhood imprisoned ARES for thir-teen months. At the age of nine, they made war on the Olympian gods, and would have piled Mt. Ossa upon Mt. Olympus and Mt. Pelion upon Mt. Ossa had they not been slain by APOLLO with his arrows.

Alp: in Teutonic folklore, the tormenting night-demon, or nightmare.

Alpheus: deity of the river of that name, which flows through Arcadia and Elis into the Ionian Sea. He pursued the NEREID ARETHUSA, who, begging ARTE-MIS to save her, was changed into a fountain in Sicily. It was believed that the river Alpheus then worked its way underground to mingle with the waters of Arethusa.

Al-Sirat: in Moslem tradition, the bridge to Paradise. It is narrower than a spider's thread and sharper than a sword, and the good pass swiftly over it, while the wicked fall down to Hell.

Amaltheia: the divine goat who suckled the infant ZEUS in Crete. In some traditions, her skin became the AEGIS. When one of Amaltheia's horns broke off, Zeus endowed it with the power of becoming filled with whatever its possessor wished, and hence it was called the "horn of plenty," or *Cornucopia*. In other traditions Amaltheia is a nymph who nourishes Zeus with the milk of a goat, and it is the goat's horn which becomes the cornucopia.

Ama-Terasu: the Japanese sun-goddess, from whom the royal family claimed descent, and whose special care was the welfare of the Mikado and his government.

Amazons: the name means "without breasts," and was given to a legendary race of warrior-women living in Asia Minor. They were ruled by a queen, and the female children had their right breasts removed to facilitate the use of the bow. Both THESEUS and HERACLES had adventures with the Amazons, and during the Trojan War they came to the assistance of Troy under their queen PENTHESILEA, who was killed by ACHILLES.

Ambrosia: meaning "not mortal," the substance considered to be, with NECTAR, the food and/or drink of the gods, continually reinforcing their immortality. Related to the Hindu AMRITA, which also confers immortality upon the gods.

Amen (Amen-Ra): originally the local god of the city of Thebes in ancient Egypt, who assumed national importance only when the kingship passed to a family of Theban nobles during the Middle Kingdom (around 2000 B.C.). After the expulsion of the Hyksos invaders under the leadership of another group of nobles from Thebes (about 1550 B.C.) and during the consequent expansion of the empire, the Egyptians ascribed all their victories to Amen and exalted him above all the other gods, equating him with RA under the name of AMEN-RA. He is usually represented in human form, wearing a flat crown surmounted by two tall, wide plumes, as does also the ithyphallic god MIN, with whose powerful generative attributes Amen was associated. Amen, with his consort MUT and their son KHONSU, make up the divine triad of Thebes.

Amentet or **Amenti:** one of the names for the afterworld in ancient Egypt, and possibly meaning "the hidden place."

Amida: one of the names of BUDDHA in Japanese myth.

Ammon: the Greek spelling of the Egyptian god AMEN.

Amor: the Latin word for "love" and used as a synonym for the god CUPID, the Greek EROS.

Amphitrite: one of the NEREIDS, and beloved of POSEIDON. She attempted to hide from him, but was discovered by a dolphin, who brought her to the lord of the sea upon his back. She is regarded as Poseidon's wife and queen of the sea, especially the Mediterranean. Their son is TRITON. She was referred to as SALACIA by the Romans.

Amphion: son of ZEUS and ANTIOPE, queen of Thebes. He and his twin brother ZETHUS, when they had grown up, marched against Thebes and conquered it, exacting a terrible revenge upon Lycus the king and DIRCE his wife, who had mistreated their mother Antiope. Amphion had been taught music by HERMES, who gave him a golden lyre. When Amphion built the walls of Thebes, he caused the stones to move into place of their own accord by the magic music of his lyre. He later married NIOBE, whose boasting of their children caused the tragic vengeance of APOLLO and ARTEMIS.

Amphitryon: king of Tiryns and husband of ALCMENE. While he was away fighting, ZEUS visited

Alcmene in the guise of Amphitryon, and she thus became the mother of HERACLES.

Amrita: in ancient Hindu myth, the food or drink which sustains the immortality of the gods, corresponding to SOMA, and perhaps the origin of the later Greek AMBROSIA.

Amshaspands: in ancient Persian myth, the six holy spirits in attendance upon AHURA-MAZDA.

Amsu: see MIN.

Anahita (Anaïtis): in ancient Persian (Zoroastrian) myth, a mother and fertility goddess sometimes regarded as the consort of MITHRA and associated with rivers, etc., as the waters of birth. She is in all probability a version of the Syro-Palestinian ANATH.

Ananke: personified Greek goddess of unalterable necessity, or fate. Her functions are related to those of the FATES, or carried out by them.

Ananta: in Hindu myth, one of the names of SESHA, ruler over the NAGAS, the mythical human serpents.

Anath (Anat): great goddess of fertility and war in ancient Syria and Palestine, the lover of the young fertility god BAAL. In the ancient Canaanite epic, Anath is Baal's chief support in his struggle with MOT (Death), and after the latter kills her lover, she proceeds against Mot, cuts him to pieces and grinds him, and then revives Baal. She has the typical ambivalent qualities of the great mother and fertility goddesses of the ancient Near East, such as ISHTAR and HATHOR.

Anchises: legendary prince of Troy who, because of his beauty, was beloved of the goddess APHRODITE and became by her the father of AENEAS. He boasted of his intercourse with the goddess, and was struck blind by a flash of lightning. During the destruction of Troy, Aeneas carried his old blind father on his shoulders from the burning city.

Andromache: wife of HECTOR, prince of Troy, and by him mother of ASTYANAX (or Scamandrius), who was hurled from the walls of Troy after its capture. Andromache was given as slave to Neoptolemus, son of ACHILLES.

Andromeda: daughter of CEPHEUS, king of Ethiopia, and his queen CASSIOPEIA. Cassiopeia had boasted that she was more beautiful than the NEREIDS, and for this POSEIDON sent a sea-dragon to lay waste the country. The oracle of AMMON (AMEN) declared that the land would be delivered only if Andromeda would be given to the dragon. Cepheus therefore chained her to a rock by the sea, but she was rescued by PERSEUS, who slew the monster when he came to ravage her. Perseus then obtained her as his wife.

Angerboda: in Norse myth, a giantess and consort of LOKI, to whom she bore FENRIR (FENRIS), JORMUNGAND and HEL.

Angus: in Celtic myth, the young god who displaced his father DAGDA from his palace. As a god of love and amorous dalliance, he had some of the qualities of the Greek EROS.

Annwn, Annwyn: in Celtic myth, the nether world and abode of the shades, ruled over by ARAWN.

Ansa: in Hindu myth, one of the ADITYAS, guardian deities of the months.

Anshar and Kishar: in ancient Sumero-Babylonian

myth, one of the pairs of vague deities who proceeded from the primordial TIAMAT and APSU. Anshar evidently means "sky-king" and Kishar "earth-king." The firstborn of Anshar was the old sky-god ANU.

Antaeus: legendary giant, son of POSEIDON and GAIA, who compelled all strangers to wrestle with him and then killed them. He was invincible as long as he remained in contact with his mother Earth, and so was slain by HERACLES, who lifted him from the ground and crushed him in mid-air.

Anteros: "return- or opposite-love"; Greek deity sometimes represented as the brother of EROS. He either struggles against love, or punishes those who do not return the love of others.

Antiope: daughter of ARES and queen of the AMAZONS and sister of HIPPOLYTE. She was carried off by THESEUS, and by him became the mother of HIPPOLYTUS.

Antu (Antum): ancient Sumerian feminine counterpart and consort of the old sky-god ANU.

Anu: ancient Sumero-Babylonian sky-god, descended from APSU (the abysmal deep) and TIAMAT (the primeval waters of Chaos). He is considered the old god, "the Father," and "King of the Gods," and as having retired to the upper heavens, leaving the ordering of the affairs of the universe to the younger generation of gods. In early times Anu was awarded a feminine counterpart, ANTU, as consort. Together with ENLIL and ENKI (or EA) he makes up the great triad of the most powerful gods.

Anubis: ancient Egyptian god associated with the mortuary cult and the afterworld, represented as a crouching jackal or as a jackal-headed man. He was patron of embalming and of the funerary rites, and in the halls of OSIRIS supervised the judgment of the deceased, whose heart was weighed against the feather of Truth.

Anunnaki: in ancient Mesopotamia, sometimes a term for the gods of the earth, as the IGIGI are those of heaven, but in some texts the positions are reversed.

Apepi: in ancient Egypt, the great serpent-dragon who is the chief of the antagonists of RA during his nocturnal journey through the underworld, and whom the sun-god continually overthrows.

Aphrodite (Lat. **Venus**): Greek goddess of love, beauty and sexual rapture. She is directly related to the ancient fertility and mother goddesses of the East, e.g. ISIS, HATHOR, ISHTAR (ASHERAH, ASTARTE), ANATH, etc., and many authorities believe that her worship came into Greece through Cyprus, one of the focal points of culture between the ancient Near East and Greece. According to the most popular account, she rose from the sea off Cyprus and established her temple there, and the Cyprian city of Paphos was in fact the site of one of the oldest centers of her worship. The same account is given of the island of Cythera, and hence she is often referred to as KYPRIS and CYTHEREA. Homer calls her the daughter of ZEUS and DIONE. According to a more widely current belief, reported by Hesiod, Aphrodite's origin goes back to the myth of the castration of OURANOS. KRONOS threw the severed genitals into the sea, which began to churn and foam about them. From this foam arose the goddess, and in the sea she was carried to Cyprus or Cythera. The Greek word *aphros*, "sea foam," was hence incorrectly explained by popular etymology as the origin of her name.

Aphrodisia, the festivals of Aphrodite, were celebrated in various centers of Greece, particularly Corinth and Athens. Her priestesses were not "prostitutes," but women who represented the goddess, and union with them was considered one of the methods of worship.

Aphrodite was officially the wife of HEPHAESTUS, but loved and was loved by many of both gods and men. Among mortals, the most famous are ADONIS and ANCHISES.

Apis: the Greek rendering of the Egyptian *Hap,* the sacred bull kept at Memphis in ancient Egypt, and regarded as an incarnation of the gods PTAH and OSIRIS. See also SERAPIS.

Apocatequil: among the Incas of Peru, the legendary high priest of the moon-god. He was god of the lightning, and statues to him were erected upon the mountaintops.

Apollo: son of ZEUS and LETO. The latter bore both Apollo and his twin sister ARTEMIS on the island of Delos, whither she had fled to escape the wrath of HERA, and Delos was one of the most ancient shrines of Apollo. Apollo assumed various functions, all broadly interrelated. He was primarily god of prophecy and vaticination, and his shrine and oracle at Delphi were famous throughout antiquity. As seer, Apollo is patron of poetry and music and leader of the MUSES, and as prophet and magician he is patron of medicine and the healing arts. Conversely, he can deal out death, and as such is represented as an archer, the "far-shooter" who slays with his arrows. He is also connected with the sun, and is after referred to as PHOEBUS, "the shining one."

Apollyon: *lit.* "the destroyer"; Greek translation of ABADDON as a personified fiend in medieval Christian demonology.

Apophis: Greek rendering of the ancient Egyptian APEPI, which see.

Apsaras: in Hindu myth, the celestial nymphs of the heaven of INDRA, similar to the HOURIS of Islam and the PERIS of ancient Persia.

Apsu: primeval Sumero-Akkadian god personifying the primordial abyss of sweet waters underneath the earth, consort of TIAMAT, the primordial abyss of the salt waters of Chaos. From Tiamat and Apsu proceeded the ensuing generations of gods, one of whom, EA (ENKI), slew Apsu and rendered helpless MUMMU, who had been the vizier of Apsu and Tiamat.

Aquilo: Latin name for the Greek BOREAS, god of the North Wind.

Arallu, Araru: in ancient Sumero-Babylonian myth, the bleak and dreary abode of the dead in the nether world, ruled over by ERESHKIGAL and NERGAL.

Arawn: in Celtic myth, the ruler over ANNWN or the nether world.

Arduina: a Gaulish moon-goddess worshipped in the Ardennes forest and identified by the Romans with DIANA.

Ares: Greek god of war, to whom the MARS of the Romans corresponded. He was the son of ZEUS and HERA, and according to Homer he inherited his mother's fierce temper and hence his delight in battles and bloodshed. He is attended by his sister ERIS ("strife, discord"), his sons DEIMOS and PHOBOS ("fear and fright") and ENYO, an old war-goddess. He personifies mainly blind, bloodthirsty rage, and is often outwitted by his rival war-deity, ATHENA, who combines wisdom and cunning with her warlike qualities. His most famous love affair is with APHRODITE, and the story of the latter's husband HEPHAESTUS catching the guilty pair *in flagrante* is delightfully told by Homer.

Arethusa: one of the NEREIDS, beloved of the river-god ALPHEUS. She begged ARTEMIS to save her from him, and was changed into a fountain bearing her name. Also the name of one of the HESPERIDES.

Argonauts: the group of heroes who sailed, under the leadership of JASON, in the ship *Argo* to fetch the golden fleece from Aeëtes, king of Colchis. The Argonauts included, among others, ORPHEUS, HERACLES, THESEUS, and the DIOSCURI.

Argus: a hundred-eyed giant whom HERA sent to guard IO after the latter had been turned into a heifer. At the command of ZEUS, HERMES slew him. Hera then took his eyes and placed them in the tail of her favorite bird, the peacock.

Ariadne: daughter of MINOS and PASIPHAË, king and queen of Crete. When THESEUS arrived at Knossos among the seven youths and seven maidens who were to be given to the MINOTAUR, Ariadne fell in love with him and supplied him with the ball of thread by which he found his way out of the LABYRINTH. Theseus, after slaying the Minotaur, escaped with his companions, taking Ariadne with him, but soon tired of her and abandoned her on the island

of Naxos. There she was found by the god DIONY-
SUS, who made her his wife.

Artemis: Greek goddess chiefly associated with the
wild life of the earth and with human birth, and
originally one of the great mother and fertility
goddesses typical of the ancient Mediterranean and
Near Eastern world. In classical times, emphasis
was placed upon her aspect of virgin huntress of
wild creatures and patroness of chastity. In her
most ancient aspects, the great goddess is at the
same time mother, virgin, mistress of wild creatures,
of fertility and desire, and fighting goddess of war,
but in many cases these attributes split off into
their component personifications: in Greece, e.g.,
as HERA and DEMETER, APHRODITE, ARTEMIS, ATHENA.
At Ephesus in Asia Minor, Artemis retained some
of her original features as Great Mother and was
represented as many-breasted (the "Diana of the
Ephesians"). Like HECATE and SELENE, she is associated with the moon, as were many of the ancient mother and fertility goddesses. In Greece,
Artemis was the daughter of ZEUS and LETO, and
twin sister of APOLLO.

Artharva Veda: one of the four groups of VEDAS, comprising magical spells.

Aruru: see NINHURSAG

Aryman: in Hindu myth, one of the ADITYAS, guardian deities of the months.

As: the singular of the plural AESIR, the great gods of
Norse myth.

Asclepius, Asklepios: see AESCULAPIUS

Asgard: in Norse myth, the city in which dwell the

AESIR, the great gods, and connected with the earth by BIFROST, the rainbow-bridge.

Asgaya Gigagei: in Cherokee Indian myth, the bisexual thunder-god, also called the Red Man and/or the Red Woman.

Asherah, Asherat: in ancient Syria and Palestine, the old mother and fertility goddess, consort of IL, and no doubt a variation of ASHTART.

Ashtart: ancient Syro-Palestinian mother and fertility goddess, analogous in her attributes and name to ISHTAR of Mesopotamia. In the ancient Caananite (Ugaritic) mythological texts, she is sometimes regarded as the consort of IL, and often closely associated with ANATH. In New Kingdom Egypt, into which both goddesses had been imported, they were often confused with each other. Ashtart is also closely connected with the sea, as is also the Greek APHRODITE, whose name, with permutations of pronunciation, came into Greek myth along with the goddess. In the ancient Near East she was also called BAALAT, "the lady," or "mistress," and KEDESHET, "the holy one." In the Old Testament her name was spelled as *Ashtoreth*, and later Greek writers on Syria mention her as *Astarte*.

Ashtoreth: see ASHTART

Ashur: patron god of ancient Assyria, assuming the roles of ENLIL and MARDUK, and god of war. He is represented as rising from a winged disc and shooting his arrows.

Ask: in Norse myth, the first human, with his wife EMBLA. They were created from trees, and became the progenitors of the human race.

Asmodeus: Latinized form of the Hebrew *Ashmedai,* prince of demons in medieval Jewish legend.

Asopus: god of the river of that name, and father of AEGINA, whom ZEUS carried off to the island named after her.

Astarte: see ASHTART

Astraea: "the star-maiden," daughter of ZEUS and THEMIS. She was, in identification with her mother, goddess of justice and lived during the Golden Age when the gods dwelled among men. When the wickedness of mankind increased, and the gods abandoned the habitations of mortals, Astraea was the last to leave, and took up her abode among the stars.

Astyanax: (or Scamandrius), infant son of HECTOR and ANDROMACHE of Troy. On the capture of Troy, he was thrown from the walls and killed, so that there would not be an heir to the throne who might restore the kingdom.

Asuras: in Hindu myth, the ruling families of the NAGAS, and possessed of divine wisdom and skill in magic, building, etc., and the power of restoring the dead.

Asvins: in Hindu myth, twins sons of SARANYU and SURYA, and known as the "Divine Physicians."

Atalanta: daughter of CLYMENE by ZEUS, or by IASUS, king of Arcadia. Exposed by her mortal father or stepfather, she was suckled by a she-bear, one of the animals of ARTEMIS, and grew up to be an athlete and huntress. She disposed of her many suitors by overcoming them in a foot race to which she challenged them with herself as the prize of victory, and killed them when they lost. She was finally conquered and married by HIPPOMENES, to whom APHRODITE had given three golden apples which he dropped one at a time in his race with Atalanta. She stopped to pick up each one, thus allowing Hippomenes to win the race.

Atar: in ancient Persian (Zoroastrian) myth, the genius of fire, and one of the YAZATAS.

Atargatis: a Hellenized form of the combination of ASHTART (ATHTART) and ANATH, the two ancient Canaanite fertility goddesses. Their orgiastic rites, in which men dressed as women and/or emasculated themselves in identification with the Great Mother (see CYBELE), penetrated throughout the Graeco-Roman world. In one of her myths current in Classical times, she was impregnated by a youth, or one of her priests, to whom she bore SEMIRAMIS, and in shame threw herself into the sea, thus accounting for her frequent representation as a beautiful woman whose lower body is that of a fish. Another usual form of her name, representing a further linguistic corruption, is DERCETO.

Atë: personification of infatuation, the rash foolishness of blind impulse, usually caused by guilt and leading to retribution. She is described as daughter of ZEUS, or of ERIS, personified goddess of strife. When she entrapped even Zeus, he hurled her down from Olympus, and she wanders over the earth, working her mischief among men.

Aten (Aton): the ancient Egyptian name for the disc of the sun itself. The Pharaoh Akhenaten (about 1370 B.C.) adopted it as the chief object of his worship in his reaction against the powerful hierarchy of AMEN of Thebes, and on many reliefs the Aten-disc is depicted ornamented with the *Uraeus*-ser-

pent and sending forth its rays ending in hands of
blessing over the king and his family. Akhenaten
held other deities in reverence also, and his Aten-
ism was definitely not monotheism, as is stated in
some of the older literature on Egypt.

Athamas: son of AEOLUS, king of Orchomenos, near
Thebes in Boeotia. At the command of HERA he
married NEPHELE, by whom he became the father
of PHRIXUS and HELLE. However, he was actually in
love with INO, daughter of CADMUS, king of Thebes,
and by her begot LEARCHUS and MELICERTES. Thus
incurring the wrath of both Hera and Nephele,
Athamas was seized with madness and slew his son
Learchus. Ino threw herself with Melicertes into
the sea, and both were changed into marine deities,
Ino becoming LEUCOTHEA (the "White Goddess")
and Melicertes PALAEMON.

Atharvan: in Hindu myth, one of the RISHIS, or legendary early sages.

Athena, Pallas Athene: Greek goddess of both war
and wisdom, with whom the Romans identified
their goddess MINERVA. According to modern
scholars she was the ancient protective goddess of
the citadel of Athens from Mycenaean times and
adopted by the invading Greeks when they conquered the city. According to the usual story of her
birth, she was the daughter of ZEUS and METIS
("wise counsel"), daughter of OCEANUS. In fear
that Metis would bear a son mightier than himself, Zeus swallowed her. The child of Metis then
grew within the head of Zeus, which HEPHAESTOS
had to cleave open with an ax. Athena then sprang
forth from the forehead of Zeus in full armor,
with helmet, shield and spear. She contended with
POSEIDON for the supremacy over Athens, and won

by producing the olive tree, which the Athenians preferred to the salt spring produced by Poseidon. Besides her armor, her usual attribute is the owl, the ancient, probably totemic, patron bird of Athens. Upon her breastplate she wears the AEGIS and the head of MEDUSA the GORGON. She is represented as being a virgin (*Parthenos*) and the Parthenon at Athens was her temple.

Athensic, Ataensic: in Iroquois Indian myth, the legendary mother of mankind who fell from Heaven into the waters of the Deluge as they receded, finding herself on the dry continent.

Athtar: ancient Arabian (pre-Islamic) god, a male version of ISHTAR, mentioned also in the Canaanite (Syro-Palestinian) mythological texts from Ugarit as son of ASHTART and as "Athtar the Terrible," possibly reflecting the war attributes of the goddess. In these texts, he is referred to as being a candidate for the rule of BAAL after the latter had been slain by MOT, but rejected as a puny weakling who could not fill Baal's throne.

Atlas: the son of the TITANS IAPETUS and CLYMENE, and brother of PROMETHEUS and EPIMETHEUS. Upon the defeat of the Titans in their war with the Olympians, Atlas was condemned to bear the heavens upon his shoulders. Hence his name, which means "bearer," or "endurer." Another tradition relates that when he refused to give shelter to PERSEUS, the latter, by means of the GORGON's head, changed him into Mt. Atlas, upon which the vault of the heavens rests.

Atman: in Hinduism, the world-soul or life principle, and the actual all-pervading Self of the universe.

Atreidae: AGAMEMNON and MENELAOS, sons of ATREUS.

Atreus: son of PELOPS and grandson of TANTALUS and father of AGAMEMNON, who became king of Mycenae, and of MENELAOS, who became king of Sparta.

Atropos: one of the three FATES. She is the Inflexible, who with her shears cuts off the thread of human life spun by CLOTHO and measured off by LACHESIS.

Attis, Atys: young fertility-deity beloved by the great earth-goddess, of the general category exemplified by ADONIS, TAMMUZ, BAAL, OSIRIS, etc. He was the beloved of CYBELE, and when he fell in love with a mortal princess, Cybele drove him mad. In his frenzy he castrated himself and the violets sprang from his blood as he died. Three days later Cybele caused his body to be resurrected. His rites were orgiastic, as were those of the other fertility religions, and during them the novitiates of his priesthood imitated his deeds by castrating themselves. Three days of sorrow followed during which his followers mourned and sought for Attis. When they found him on the third day, there followed a period of wild rejoicing.

Atum (Tum, Temu): *lit.* "he who completes, or perfects," an aspect of the ancient Egyptian god RA, which see.

Atys: see ATTIS.

Audhumla: in Norse myth the primeval cow on whose milk the giant YMIR was fed.

Aurora: Roman goddess of the dawn, identified with the Greek EOS.

Auster: in Latin, the south, or properly the southwest, wind which brought fogs and rain or sultry heat. It is the modern *sirocco*.

Autonoë: daughter of CADMUS and mother of AC-
TAEON. With her sisters INO and AGAVE she tore the
latter's son PENTHEUS to pieces during their Bacchic
rage.

Avalon: in the Arthurian legends, the "Place of Apples," the paradisiacal island to which the dying
Arthur was taken.

Avatar: in Hindu myth, the term applied to the
various incarnations of the gods BRAHMA and
VISHNU.

Avesta: see ZEND-AVESTA

Awonawilona: chief god of the Zuni Indians of New
Mexico, regarded as father and creator of all.

Azazel: in the Old Testament, a wild demon of the
desert to whom the scapegoat was driven forth,
and whose name probably means "goat-god." In
Moslem theology, he is a JINN and analogous to
the DEVIL in refusing to acknowledge the supremacy
of God.

Azrael: in Islam, the angel of death.

B

Ba: in ancient Egyptian theology, the soul of man which is within him while he lives and which leaves him after the death of his body. It is represented as a man-headed hawk, and is usually present at the judgment of the deceased before OSIRIS.

Baal: *lit.* "lord, master," in ancient Syro-Palestinian (Canaanite) myth the young and powerful fertility god whose attributes are the lightning and the rainstorm and the generative forces of nature. He is the main protagonist, with the goddess ANATH, his lover and consort, in the mythological texts of Ugarit. He is slain by MOT (Death) and resurrected by Anath, thus being analogous to the other dying and resurrected fertility-gods of the ancient world, such as OSIRIS, TAMMUZ/ADONIS and ZAGREUS/DIONYSUS. At Ugarit he was also referred to as ALIYN BAAL, probably "Baal the Powerful," and *Zevul Baal,* "Prince Baal." The latter title was perverted, with pejorative intent, by the Old Testament writers into BEELZEBUB, which see.

Baalath: in the Semitic languages, "the Lady," an epithet of the goddess ASHTART.

Baal Shamin: in Syrian Semitic, *lit.* "the lord of the heavens," one of the appellations of BAAL.

Baba: ancient Sumerian fertility-goddess of the city of Lagash, patroness of the king and consort of NINGIRSU. Her name was formerly read incorrectly as BAU.

Babbar: ancient Sumerian sun-god, corresponding to the Babylonian SHAMASH.

Bacabs: in Mayan myth, agricultural and fertility deities who also upheld the sky at its cardinal points.

Bacchae or **Bacchantes:** an epithet of the MAENADS, the frenzied, ecstatic women in the train of DIONYSUS.

Bacchus: the most frequent epithet of DIONYSUS, and the name by which he is called in Roman literature, in addition to LIBER.

Badb: in Celtic myth, a war-goddess, "the crow," who haunts the battlefield, inciting to battle and causing confusion among the warriors with her magic.

Balder, Baldur: in Norse myth, the son of ODIN and FRIGG, the most beautiful of the AESIR, and a god of light, wisdom and righteousness. He was killed by his brother HOD at the instigation of LOKI but will return again at the final destruction of the world.

Banshee, Benshee: in Celtic myth, one of the *Bean-Sidhe,* "daughters of the hill folk," the fairy people who live within the hills of Ireland.

Basilisk: a mythical serpent or lizard whose look and breath were fatal.

Bassarids: from *bassaris,* "foxskin," worn by DIONYSUS in his Thracian mysteries. Hence the Thracian Dionysus was sometimes called Bassareus, and his MAENADS *Bassarids.*

Bast: see BASTET

Bastet (Bast): beneficent goddess of ancient Egypt,

represented as a cat or as a cat-headed woman, whose rituals and processions were rather licentious. Because of her feline associations, she was sometimes regarded as the beneficent aspect of the fierce and destructive lioness-headed goddess SEKHMET.

Bau: former, erroneous reading of the name of the Mesopotamian goddess BABA, which see.

Beelzebub: in Hebrew, *Baal-zevuv*, usually interpreted as "Lord of Flies" and taken as an epithet of Satan in medieval theology. Actually the term is a deliberate mocking perversion of the Canaanite *Baal-Zebul*, "Prince Baal," one of the standard titles by which the pagan god BAAL was called.

Bel: *lit.* "lord, master," the ancient Mesopotamian appellation of ENLIL and MARDUK, linguistically the same as BAAL.

Bellerophon: legendary prince and hero of Corinth. When he was the guest of King Proetus of Argos, Antea the queen attempted to seduce him, but he repulsed her advances. Enraged, she accused him to Proetus of attempting to seduce her and Proetus sent him to Iobates, king of Lycia, with a sealed letter requesting him to put the bearer to death. Iobates sent him to fight the monster CHIMAERA, but with the assistance of ATHENA he caught the winged horse PEGASUS, and with its help slew the Chimaera. Later he attempted to ascend to heaven upon Pegasus, but fell off its back to the earth, while Pegasus flew on to heaven and dwells among the stars.

Bellona: Roman goddess of war, from the Latin *bellum*, "war." She is sometimes regarded as the sis-

ter or wife of MARS, and identified with the Greek
ENYO.

Beltia: see ZARPANIT

Beltis: Greek rendering of *Belit,* the feminine of BEL
and an appellation of NINLIL/NINHURSAG.

Belus: son of POSEIDON by Libya, daughter of
EPAPHUS, who was the son of IO and ZEUS. Belus's
most famous sons were AEGYPTUS and DANAÜS. He
is associated with Babylon and Assyria, and his
name is no doubt an echo of the Canaanite god
BAAL.

Bendis: Thracian mother and fertility goddess, identified with the moon and with HECATE, ARTEMIS and
PERSEPHONE, and invested with power over heaven
and earth.

Benten: Japanese sea-goddess of benevolent aspect,
believed to have captivated and then espoused a
serpent-dragon who had been devouring children.

Berserks: "the bearskin-people," in Norse myth, wild,
warlike beings who are subject to ferocious rages
during which they might kill their own people or
fight with the boulders or timbers of the forest.

Bes: bandy-legged dwarf god of ancient Egypt, depicted as nude, with prominent genitals, and with
the ears, mane and tail of a lion or cat, or wearing
the skin of a feline animal and sometimes a row of
feathers about his head. He was a god of human
pleasures and jollity, music and childbirth, and
was very popular, principally among the masses of
the common people.

Bhaga: in Hindu myth, one of the ADITYAS, guardian
deities of the months. He was blinded by VIRA-

BHADRA, the monster created by SHIVA.

Bhavani: in Hindu myth, one of the terrible aspects of PARVATI, consort of SHIVA. See DURGHA and KALI.

Bia: in Greek myth, personification of brute force, son of PALLAS and STYX and brother of ZELUS and NIKE.

Bifrost: in Norse myth, the rainbow-bridge which connects the earth with ASGARD, the city of the gods.

Bimbo-Gami: Japanese god of poverty.

Bishamon: Japanese war-god also regarded as a giver of wealth and good fortune, and as a guardian of one of the four cardinal points (the North).

Bona Dea: in Latin, "the good goddess." An ancient Roman goddess of the earth and of fertility, and described as the sister, wife or daughter of FAUNUS, being herself called FAUNA, as well as OPS, "plenty," and TELLUS, "earth." Like the very ancient great goddesses, she presided over both virginity and fertility in women, and at her festivals in Rome, conducted by both VESTALS and matrons, no man was allowed to be present. Consecrated serpents were kept in her temple at Rome, indicating her phallic nature.

Book of the Dead: the collection of ancient Egyptian magic formulae, prayers, hymns, etc., which was buried with the mummy of the deceased, and possession of which was believed to enable him to pass successfully through the trials besetting him on his journey into the afterworld, and to be justified before OSIRIS and become identified with him. The name of this collection in ancient Egyptian was *The Chapters of Coming Forth by Day*. The Arab tomb-pillagers of modern times called the scrolls which they found with the mummies "The Book of the Dead," and the term has persisted.

Boötes: son of DEMETER and IASION, and brother of PLUTUS. He invented the plow, to which he attached a team of oxen, and was the first to cultivate the soil. Demeter placed him, with his plow and oxen, among the stars as the constellation BOÖTES, "the ox-driver."

Boreas: Greek god of the North Wind, son of the TITAN Astraeus and EOS, and brother of EURUS, ZEPHYRUS and NOTUS. In Latin, AQUILO.

Borr: in Norse myth, son of BURI and father of ODIN, VILI and VE.

Bragi: in Norse myth, one of the AESIR and son of ODIN. He is god of eloquence and the art of poetry, and patron of bards. His consort is IDUN, goddess of eternal youth.

Brahma: in Hindu myth, the senior member of the triad, or TRIMURTI, of the great gods Brahma, VISHNU and SHIVA. In later times he became symbolized as the supreme eternal deity whose essence pervades the entire universe.

Brahmanspati: in Hindu myth, the "lord of prayer," also regarded as the father of AGNI.

Briareus: one of the HEKATONCHEIRES, the hundred-armed GIANTS. When HERA, POSEIDON, and ATHENA wished to bind ZEUS, THETIS called him to the latter's aid, and he drove them off. See AEGAEON.

Brigit: in Celtic myth, the triple goddess of the hearth, childbirth, abundance and poetic inspiration.

Briseis: in the *Iliad,* a captive awarded to ACHILLES

as spoils of war. She was seized from him by AGA-MEMNON as compensation for his loss of the captive CHRYSEIS, who had to be returned to her father. This was the cause of the wrath of Achilles and his feud with Agamemnon, which is the subject of the *Iliad*.

Britomartis: ancient Cretan fertility and nature goddess, identified with the Hellenic ARTEMIS and, like her, patroness of hunters. Like many of the ancient goddesses, she was associated with the sea, and hence also patroness of fishermen and sailors. She was assimilated to another Cretan goddess, DICTYNNA, and was often so called.

Bromios: "the thunderer," or "he of the loud shout," an epithet of DIONYSUS.

Brunhild: see BRYNHILD

Brynhild, Brunhild: in Norse myth, a princess loved and betrothed by SIGURD. When he was slain, she had herself burned on his funeral pyre. The later Teutonic version of the story represents her as a VALKYRIE awakened by Sigurd from an enchanted sleep.

Buddha: *lit.* "the enlightened one," although represented in the VEDAS as the ninth incarnation (AVATAR) of VISHNU, is regarded by his followers as not a god at all, but as a mortal prince called Gautama, of miraculous birth, who renounced his princely life for one of asceticism. He taught that the miseries inherent in the life of the endless transmigrations of the soul can be obviated by defeating the desires which cause them (KARMA). Once this is done, the state of release called NIRVANA is attained.

Buri: in Norse myth, the god who sprang from the divine COW AUDHUMLA and who was father of BORR and grandfather of ODIN.

Buto: the patron goddess of Lower Egypt (the Delta of the Nile) symbolized by the *uraeus*-serpent or cobra, and depicted as a woman, or as a cobra with the crown of Lower Egypt on its head.

C

Cabala: see KABBALAH

Cabiri: properly the Greek *Kabeiroi,* deities of Phrygian origin connected with fertility, and later identified with the CORYBANTES and KOURETES (CURETES). They were the subject of a mystery cult celebrated throughout the Graeco-Roman world, but centered principally on the island of Samothrace. As chthonic and fertility deities they were sometimes associated with HEPHAESTUS as metal-craftsmen, and with RHEA, HECATE, DEMETER and PERSEPHONE.

Cacus: in Roman myth, a fire-spitting giant, son of VULCAN, who dwelt near the future site of Rome and plundered the countryside. When HERCULES came there with the cattle of GERYON, Cacus stole some of them while the hero was sleeping, dragging them to his cave backward by their tails so that their tracks would point in the opposite direction. The lowing of the cattle, however, betrayed their presence in the cave to Hercules and he retrieved them and slew Cacus.

Cadmus: son of Agenor, king of Tyre in Phoenicia, and brother of EUROPA. When the latter was carried off over the sea by ZEUS who had approached her in the form of a bull, Agenor sent Cadmus to search for her. Unsuccessful, Cadmus consulted the Delphic oracle, and was told to follow a certain cow to the spot where she would stop to rest, and there he was to build a city. Cadmus did so, and followed the cow to Boeotia, where he founded the city of Thebes and became its first king. He slew a dragon who guarded a sacred well, and sowed its teeth in the ground at the command of ATHENA. Immediately armed men sprang up from the dragon's teeth, and began to fight each other. Of them five survived, becoming legendary ancestors of the Thebans. He was given as wife HARMONIA, daughter of ARES and APHRODITE, and became by her the father of INO, SEMELE, AGAVE, and AUTONOË. In their old age, Cadmus and Harmonia were changed into immortal serpents. Cadmus is credited with having introduced into Greece the Semitic alphabet used in Phoenicia, from which the Greek and later Roman alphabets were derived.

Caduceus: the herald's staff or wand of HERMES, and usually depicted as a winged rod with two serpents intertwined about it. As a group of fertility symbols, it is emblematic of the magic potency of the deity, and of the prosperity of peace.

Calchas: see KALCHAS

Calliope: Greek Muse of epic poetry, usually represented with a scroll or tablets and stylus. See MUSES.

Calypso: a sea nymph who inhabited the island of Ogygia, upon which ODYSSEUS was wrecked. He spent eight years with her, and she tried to persuade him to stay with the promise of immortality and eternal youth. But Odysseus longed for his home, and Calypso was compelled to release him at the command of ZEUS.

Camazotz: the bat-god of the Central American Indians, figuring in the legendary Struggles of the early gods and peoples and ultimately defeated.

Camenae: ancient Italian nymphs of springs and fountains, sometimes identified by the Romans with the Greek MUSES.

Camulus: Gaulish god mentioned by the Romans, who associated him with MARS.

Canopic Jars: in ancient Egypt, the four clay jars in which the embalmed entrails of the deceased were placed. They were then put into a chest and deposited in the tomb together with the mummified body. Each was under the protection of one of the four "Sons of Horus," the covers of the jars being carved to represent their heads: 1) MESTI, human-headed, guarding the liver; 2) HAPY, ape-headed, guarding the lungs; 3) DUAMUTEF, jackal-headed, guarding the stomach; and 4) KEBEHSENUF, falcon-headed, guarding the intestines. The entire Canopic Chest was protected by the four goddesses ISIS, NEPHTHYS, NEITH and SELKET. See CANOPUS.

Canopus: in Greek myth, the pilot of MENELAOS, buried at Canopus at one of the mouths of the

Nile, and said to be worshipped in the form of a jar with a human head which spouted streams of water upon the fire which the Chaldeans had built around it when they wanted to destroy it. The Greeks obviously made this association with the jars in which the embalmed entrails of the deceased were placed in ancient Egypt, and these are referred to today as CANOPIC JARS.

Carmenta: ancient Roman prophetic goddess who protected women in childbirth.

Cassandra: daughter of PRIAM, king of Troy, and HECUBA his queen. She was beloved of APOLLO, who conferred the gift of prophecy upon her on the condition that she yield herself to him. When she had been endowed with the prophetic art she refused to keep her promise, and Apollo who, like all gods, could not withdraw what he had ordained, decreed that she should predict truly, but that no one would ever believe her prophecies. On the capture of Troy, she was seized from the sanctuary of ATHENA and violated by AJAX. On the division of the spoils, she fell to the lot of AGAMEMNON, who took her back with him to Mycenae, where she was slain by CLYTEMNESTRA.

Cassiopeia: wife of CEPHEUS, king of Ethiopia, mother of ANDROMEDA. She boasted of being more beautiful than the NEREIDS, and in retaliation POSEIDON sent a sea-monster to ravage the country. See ANDROMEDA and PERSEUS.

Castor: brother of POLLUX and one of the "Heavenly Twins." See DIOSCURI.

Cecrops: legendary founder and first king of Athens, half man and half serpent, and born of the soil. In his reign POSEIDON and ATHENA contended for the lordship of Attica, and Cecrops decided in favor of the goddess. The citadel, or Acropolis, of Athens was named Cecropia in his honor.

Celaeno: one of the three HARPIES.

Centaurs: a mythical race of wild creatures, half men and half horse, who roamed Mt. Pelion in Thessaly.

Cepheus: legendary king of Ethiopia, son of BELUS. He was husband of CASSIOPEIA, and father of ANDROMEDA.

Cerberus: the terrible dog which guarded the entrance to Hades. He was originally described as having fifty or a hundred heads, but was later pictured as having only three, with the tail of a serpent.

Ceridwen: ancient British fertility and mother goddess, who possessed a cauldron in which she prepared a magic draught which conferred knowledge and inspiration upon the drinker.

Ceto: daughter of OCEANUS and GAIA, and by PHORCYS the mother of the PHORCYDES.

Ceres: Roman goddess corresponding to the Greek DEMETER.

Chaos: the vast, abysmal deep which existed even before the creation of the universe and the gods, and out of which all created things, including the gods, proceeded.

Charites: the Greek name for the GRACES.

Charon: ancient Greek underworld deity, son of EREBUS, who ferries the shades of the dead in his boat across the river STYX to the realms of HADES.

He must be paid his fare, and for this purpose a small coin (an obolus) was placed in the mouth of the deceased before burial.

Charybdis: see SCYLLA

Chemosh: god of the ancient Moabites mentioned in the Old Testament, possibly identified with the Mesopotamian SHAMASH.

Cherubim: winged creatures mentioned in the book of Ezekiel in the Bible as bearing the throne and chariot of the Deity, and hence later conceived of as a type of angels. Actually, they were a lesser order of ancient Mesopotamian deities—winged and human-headed bulls who guarded the gates of the royal palace.

Chimaera: a fire-breathing legendary monster, part lion, part goat and part dragon, who ravaged the country about Lycia in Asia Minor and was finally killed by BELLEROPHON.

Chiron: the wise and just among the CENTAURS, the others being wild and uncivilized. He was the son of the OCEANID PHILYRA and KRONOS, who in fear of the jealousy of RHEA, transformed himself into a stallion and Philyra into a mare, and so their son Chiron was half man, half horse. He was instructed by APOLLO and ARTEMIS in the arts of music, medicine, prophecy, hunting, etc., and in turn was the teacher of the various great Achaean heroes such as Jason, Achilles, etc., and taught AESCULAPIUS the arts of medicine. While hunting with the other Centaurs, he was struck by one of the poisoned arrows of HERACLES, and although immortal did not wish to bear the pain, and giving up his immortality to PROMETHEUS, he died. ZEUS placed him among the stars as the constellation Sagittarius, the Archer.

Chloris: Greek goddess, personification of Spring, and so identified with the Roman FLORA. As divinity of blossoming flowers, she is the spouse of ZEPHYRUS.

Chryseis: in the *iliad*, daughter of Chryses, priest of APOLLO at a town near Troy. She was captured in a raid by the Achaeans and awarded as spoils of war to AGAMEMNON. Chryses came to the Achaean camp to ransom his daughter, but was rudely refused by Agamemnon. Thereupon Apollo sent a plague which ravished the camps of the Achaeans, to cease only when Agamemnon returned Chryseis. His forcible seizure, as compensation, of ACHILLES' captive BRISEIS caused the feud between the two leaders which is the subject of the *Iliad.*

Circe: daughter of HELIOS and an OCEANID, and sister of AEËTES, king of Colchis, and PASIPHAË. Circe was famed for her magic arts and potions, and changed all men who visited the island where she dwelt into swine by having them taste of the contents of her magic cup. When ODYSSEUS and his companions were cast upon her island, she transformed Odysseus's men into swine, but Odysseus himself was given by HERMES the magic herb *moly* which protected him from the spell. He remained a year with Circe, and she became by him the mother of Telegonus, the founder of Tusculum in Italy.

Clio: Greek Muse of history, usually represented with scroll or set of tablets. See MUSES.

Cloacina: from the Latin *cloaca,* "sewer." She is regarded as the deity presiding over the system of sewers which drained the refuse of the city of

Rome. The main sewer was called the *Cloaca Maxima*.

Clotho: one of the three FATES. She is the Spinner, who with her distaff spins the thread of human life.

Clymene: daughter of OCEANUS and TETHYS. By the TITAN IAPETUS she became the mother of ATLAS, PROMETHEUS, and EPIMETHEUS.

Clytemnestra: daughter of TYNDAREUS and LEDA—or according to another tradition, of Leda by ZEUS, who visited her in the form of a swan—and sister of CASTOR, POLLUX and HELEN. She became the wife of AGAMEMNON, and by him the mother of ORESTES, IPHIGENIA and ELECTRA. During Agamemnon's absence at Troy, she became the adulterous paramour of AEGISTHUS, and upon Agamemnon's return murdered him with the aid of Aegisthus, giving as excuse Agamemnon's sacrifice of Iphigenia. Clytemnestra and Aegisthus were later slain by Orestes in revenge for his father's murder, of which he was apprised by his sister Electra.

Cockatrice: mythical classical serpent hatched by a reptile from a cock's egg, and believed to be able to kill with its glance.

Cocytus: "the river of wailing," one of the mythical rivers which ran through the realms of HADES.

Coelus: the Latin for "sky," and personified god of the heavens. As such, he was identified with the Greek OURANOS, and was husband of TERRA, "earth."

Consentes (Consentes Dii, Dii Consentes): the twelve gods of the Etruscans, called the PENATES of the Thunderer himself (i.e. JUPITER), considered by the Romans to be fierce and awesome primal divinities. The Romans later identified them with the Greek Olympians.

Consus: primitive Roman deity, originally presiding over the storing of grain, later regarded as god of secret counsels and also identified with NEPTUNE.

Coronis: legendary Thessalian princess, and by APOLLO the mother of AESCULAPIUS. She was killed by ARTEMIS for her unfaithfulness to Apollo, but the latter snatched the unborn Aesculapius from the flames of her funeral pyre and had him brought up by the CENTAUR CHIRON, who instructed him in all the healing arts.

Corybantes: the attendants upon the Phrygian RHEA CYBELE, who accompanied her with wild, orgiastic music and dancing, clashing their cymbals and sounding their pipes in her train on her nocturnal wanderings by torchlight over the mountains. During their wild orgies they cut their flesh with knives, as did the actual priests of CYBELE, who were self-castrated in identification with the goddess.

Cottus: one of the HEKATONCHEIRES, the hundred-armed GIANTS.

Cotytto or **Cotys:** ancient Thracian mother and fertility goddess, and later identified with RHEA CYBELE. Her rites, like those of all the primitive goddesses, were orgiastic in nature, and celebrated with much licentiousness.

Cumaean Sibyl: the earliest of the SIBYLS, who was said to have come from the East and resided at Cumae. It was she who sold the SIBYLLINE BOOKS to TARQUIN.

Creation Epic (Babylonian): the Babylonian ac-

count of creation celebrating the destruction of
TIAMAT, goddess of CHAOS and the primeval watery
abyss, by the young god MARDUK and his subsequent creation and ordering of the Cosmos. The
epic is usually called *Enuma Elish,* meaning "when
above," from the opening words of the first lines,
"When above the heavens were not yet named,
etc."

Crom Cruaich: in ancient Irish myth, a god of destruction to whom the firstborn of animals and the
chief scions of the clans were sacrificed.

Cronus: see KRONOS

Cupid: from the Latin *Cupido,* "desire." The Roman
name for the Greek god EROS.

Curetes: see KOURETES

Cybele: great fertility goddess of Asia Minor, whose
worship was adopted by the Greeks in Lydia and
Phrygia, who identified her with RHEA. Her rites
spread over the Roman world, where she was
known as the *Magna Mater,* "the great mother"
(of the gods). Following the usual pattern of
chthonic goddess religions, her son ATTIS figured
prominently in her rites, which were ecstatic and
orgiastic in nature. During the course of these, the
novitiates among her devotees emasculated themselves, following the example of Attis in the myth,
and to achieve identification and union with the
goddess.

Cyclopes: giants who were so called because they had
one round eye in the middle of their foreheads.
According to Hesiod, they were TITANS, and sons
of OURANOS and GAIA. They were thrown into TAR-
TARUS by KRONOS, but were later released by ZEUS

and worked at forging his thunderbolts. By association, they were later regarded as assisting HEPHAESTUS at his forge, which lay beneath Aetna or neighboring volcanoes. Homer considers them a race of giants who devour men and hold Zeus of no regard. The best-known Cyclopes is POLYPHEMUS, who was blinded by ODYSSEUS.

Cynthia: an epithet of ARTEMIS, referring to her birthplace and that of her twin brother APOLLO on Mt. Cynthus on the island of Delos.

Cytherea: an epithet of APHRODITE, as having appeared from the sea off the island of Cythera.

D

Dactyls: legendary deities associated with Mt. Ida in Phrygia. To them was ascribed the discovery of iron and the art of working metals by fire.

Daedalus: legendary master craftsman associated with Crete. He made the wooden cow for PASIPHAË, and after the birth of the MINOTAUR, fashioned the LABYRINTH in which the monster was confined. In order to escape from Crete, Daedalus made wings of feathers for himself and his son ICARUS, and they flew out over the Aegaean. Icarus, however, flew too near the sun, the wax melted, and he fell into the sea and was drowned.

Daemon (Daimon, Demon): from the Greek *Daimon*, a term originally denoting the deities in general, but later and more generally used for intermediate or lesser gods, and for the GENIUS. Under the influence of medieval Christianity, they became evil spirits.

Dagan: *lit.* "grain" in the Semitic dialect of ancient Syria and Palestine, an appellation of BAAL.

Dagda: in Celtic myth, *lit.* "the good god," called "the father," omnipotent and omniscient, being a formidable fighter, magician and artisan. He is also a fertility god, possessing a cauldron which continually supplies food in abundance, and unites in sacred marriage with the MORRIGAN.

Dagon: Hebrew spelling of the name of the god worshipped by the Philistines, properly DAGAN, which see.

Daikoku: Japanese god of fertility and wealth and craftsmanship represented as bearing a hammer with male and female symbols. His animal is the rat.

Daityas: in Hindu myth, the early giants who fought against the gods.

Daksha: in Hindu myth, one of the ADITYAS, guardian deities of the months. He was the father-in-law of SHIVA, who, as a result of a quarrel, sent his monster VIRABHADRA to cut off Daksha's head, which was replaced by that of a goat or ram.

Damkina: ancient Sumero-Babylonian goddess, consort of ENKI (EA).

Dana, Danu: ancient Celtic mother-goddess of one of the legendary early peoples of Ireland, the TUATHA DE DANANN, "Tribes of the Goddess Dana."

Danaë: daughter of ACRISIUS, king of Argos. An oracle had predicted that Danaë would bear a son who would kill his grandfather. Acrisius therefore confined her within a brazen tower, but there she was impregnated by ZEUS, who visited her in the form of a shower of gold. Thus she became the mother of PERSEUS. Acrisius shut up Danaë and her son into a chest, which was thrown into the sea. The chest was borne to the island of Seriphos, and its king, Polydectes, later attempted to force Danaë to marry him, sending Perseus off on his adventures in order to get him out of the way.

Danaïdes: the fifty daughters of DANAÜS who fled with them to Argos in fear of his brother AEGYPTUS. The fifty sons of Aegyptus followed them to Argos and forced Danaüs to give them his daughters in marriage. At their father's behest they murdered their husbands on their wedding night, all except HYPERMNESTRA, who spared her husband LYNCEUS. In Hades the Danaïdes were condemned eternally to pour water into a vessel with holes in its bottom.

Danaüs: twin brother of AEGYPTUS and son of BELUS. In consequence of a quarrel with Aegyptus over the assignment of territory, Danaüs with his fifty daughters (the DANAÏDES) fled to Argos, where he was made king.

Daphne: Greek nymph, daughter of the river-god PENEUS. She was pursued by APOLLO, and prayed that he might never possess her. She was thereupon transformed into a laurel, which became the favorite tree of Apollo.

Dea Syria: Latin for "the Syrian goddess," thus referred to in Roman times, when her worship, with that of the other ancient mother and fertility goddesses of the ancient Near East (e.g. ISIS) had become popular throughout the Roman Empire. Specifically, she is ATARGATIS.

Deianira: legendary ancient Greek princess who became the wife of HERACLES after he fought for her with the bull-shaped ACHELOUS, whom he vanquished. She unwittingly gave Heracles the poisoned shirt of the CENTAUR NESSUS, causing her husband's death, and killed herself for grief.

Deimos: "fear," sometimes considered as a son of ARES, and accompanying him in battle.

Deino: one of the GRAIAE, and daughter of PHORCYS and CETO.

Deirdre, Derdriu: in Celtic myth, the beautiful daughter of one of the bards, whose birth and the many deaths she was to cause were prophesied by a druid. The child was to be killed at birth, but she was ordered spared by the king and reared apart. When she was grown, the king claimed her as a wife and had her lovers slain, in revenge for which there was occasioned great slaughter. Deirdre refused to be comforted by the king and killed herself.

Demeter: Greek earth-goddess *par excellence*, who brings forth the fruits of the earth, particularly the various grains. In the systematized theology, she was the daughter of KRONOS and RHEA and sister of ZEUS by whom she became the mother of PERSEPHONE. Demeter was the great goddess of the *Eleusinian Mysteries,* the ritual of which was founded upon the myth of the abduction of Persephone by HADES. Demeter wandered over the earth in search of her, and during this time the earth brought forth no grain. Demeter was kindly received by the king of Eleusis, who according to later legend sent forth his son TRIPTOLEMOS to teach the arts of agriculture to men. Zeus finally sent HERMES down to the nether world, ordering Hades to restore Persephone to her mother, so that the earth might bring forth once more. However, since Persephone had eaten a pomegranate (a common fertility symbol) which Hades had given her, she had to spend a third of the year with her husband in the infernal regions. Demeter's usual symbolic attributes are the fruits of the earth and the torch, the latter presumably referring to her search for Persephone. Her great festival, the *Thesmophoria*, was celebrated in Athens and other centers in Greece, and throughout Classical times members of all social strata came from all parts of the Mediterranean world to be initiated in and celebrate her Mysteries at Eleusis.

Demiurge, Demiourgos: in the dualistic Gnostic theology, the creator of the material world, which is evil by nature. Hence he was identified by the early Christian Gnostic heretics with YAHWEH.

Demogorgon: a confused medieval rendering of the DEMIURGE.

Demon: see DAEMON

Dendrites: *lit.* "he of the tree," an epithet of DIONYSUS as fertility-god.

Derceto (Dercetis): corruption of the name of the Hellenized Canaanite goddess ATARGATIS.

Deucalion: son of PROMETHEUS and CLYMENE. He married PYRRHA, daughter of EPIMETHEUS, and when ZEUS destroyed the degenerate first race of men by a flood, Deucalion and Pyrrha were saved because of their piety. On the advice of his father, Deucalion built an ark and after the flood he and Pyrrha left the ark and gave thank offerings to Zeus. Upon inquiring of the oracle of THEMIS as to how the earth might be replenished with men, they were told to throw the bones of their mother behind them. Realizing that the mother of all is the earth, they took stones and cast them behind them. The stones thrown by Deucalion became men, and those thrown by Pyrrha, women.

Deva: in Hinduism, the generic term for a divine being, degraded into an evil spirit in Zoroastrianism.

Devi: *lit. "the* goddess," in Hindu myth, an appellation of PARVATI, the consort of SHIVA and considered as his potent, dynamic energy (SHAKTI). Like all ancient mother and fertility goddesses, she is ambivalent in her nature, in her benevolent aspect being called UMA, "light," and HAIMAVATI as being born of the Himalaya mountains, and in her malignant and destructive aspect DURGA, "the inaccessible," and KALI, "the black one." Her symbol is the YONI, the female generative organ.

Devil: along with *diable, teufel,* etc., in the European languages, a corruption of the Greek *diabolos,* "adversary, prosecutor," which is in turn a translation of the Hebrew SATAN. Also used in the plural, in medieval theology, to denote Satan's attending demons.

Dhatri: in Hindu myth, one of the ADITYAS, guardian deities of the months.

Diana: ancient Roman nature-goddess, patroness of

fertility and childbirth and closely identified with the Greek ARTEMIS.

Dictynna: ancient Cretan nature and fertility goddess, and often identified with BRITOMARTIS, another Cretan goddess, and like her identified with the Hellenic ARTEMIS. To account for the name *Dictynna* it was related that MINOS pursued her, and she escaped him by leaping from a cliff into the sea, but was caught by a fisherman's net (*dictyon*) and saved.

Dido: legendary founder and queen of Carthage, daughter of BELUS and sister of PYGMALION. In Vergil, she entertained AENEAS, who arrived at Carthage during his wanderings, and fell in love with him. When he left her to continue his search for his new home in Italy, she destroyed herself on a funeral pyre.

Dike: ancient Greek personified goddess of justice, one of the three HORAE, and daughter of ZEUS and THEMIS.

Dione: an ancient goddess or Titaness who, according to one tradition, was the mother of APHRODITE by ZEUS. Actually, her name is a feminine form of Zeus (*Dios*).

Dionysus: Greek god of the awesome potency and teeming fertility of nature, and of the divine ecstasy inspired by surrender to and union with these powerful and irrational forces of generation. Through participation in his orgiastic rites, the worshipper felt within himself such a surging vitality resulting from this communion with the great life forces that he felt himself born anew. The ecstasy was induced by wild dancing and by wine. Hence wine and the vine became his most common symbols, as a typical product of the fertility of the earth, and capable of inducing a heightened state of awareness and a temporary release from the inhibitions necessitated by society. The bull, the goat and the serpent, powerful fertility symbols to all ancient peoples, are the animals associated with him. He is represented as carrying the *thyrsus,* a long staff crowned with a clump of vine leaves or a pinecone, obvious phallic symbols. Other symbols of generation such as certain fruits, the ceremonial basket (*liknos*), as well as the phallus itself, were carried in his cult processions.

Dionysus was the son of ZEUS and of SEMELE the daughter of CADMUS, founder and king of Thebes. HERA persuaded the pregnant Semele to persuade Zeus to appear before her in all his divine glory. Unwillingly, Zeus appeared to her in his bolts of lightning, and Semele was engulfed in the flames. Zeus, however, took her child and sewed him up in his thigh, from which the infant Dionysus was born. He traveled through Asia, Syria and Egypt as well as the Mediterranean world, introducing his rites, and incidentally taking as his bride ARIADNE, daughter of MINOS of Crete, who had been abandoned by THESEUS on the island of Naxos. His most frequent epithet is BACCHUS, and he is so termed in Roman literature.

Many aspects of his worship partook of the nature of a secret cult, into which the worshipper was initiated, and it was through the ritual the initiate was reborn and promised the blessings of eternal life and/or potency. These secret rites were known as the *Mysteries.* Other deities had their Mysteries also: DEMETER, ZEUS, the CABEIRI and ORPHEUS. The Mysteries of Orpheus were later assimilated to those of Dionysus.

Associated with Dionysus in the myths are SILE-NUS, PAN, the SATYRS, the NYMPHS, and his wildly ecstatic priestesses, the MAENADS.

Dioscuri: in Greek, *Dios kouroi*, "the youths of Zeus," and referring to the brothers CASTOR and POLLUX. According to one tradition, ZEUS rewarded them for their faithfulness to each other by placing them among the stars as the constellation Gemini, the "Heavenly Twins." They were the children of LEDA by Zeus and/or TYNDAREUS, king of Sparta and Leda's husband (see LEDA). They rescued their sister HELEN, who in her youth was abducted by THESEUS of Athens, and later took part in the expedition of the Argonauts. They are usually represented as horsemen, athletes and warriors. They were sometimes identified with the CABIRI.

Dirae: A Latin name for the FURIES.

Dirce: wife, after ANTIOPE, of LYCUS, king of Thebes. She treated Antiope cruelly and was later punished by Antiope's sons, AMPHION and ZETHUS, who tied her to the horns of a bull, by whom she was dragged to death.

Dis: or DISPATER, a contraction of the Latin *Dives,* "the wealthy," *Dives Pater,* "the wealthy father," or "Father Wealth," ancient Roman ruler of the underworld. The name corresponds to the Greek PLUTO, PLOUTOS, also meaning "wealth," and referring to the wealth of precious stones and metals to be found below the earth. In classical Roman times, the deity corresponded to the Greek HADES, which see.

Discordia: personified Roman goddess of strife, corresponding to the Greek ERIS.

Dithyrambos: a frequent epithet of DIONYSUS, and

possibly meaning "he of the double door," i.e.
twice-born, alluding to his premature birth from
SEMELE and then from the thigh of ZEUS. The term
also refers to the solemn odes or hymns sung to
Dionysus at his festivals.

Donar: in Teutonic myth, god of thunder and warlike strength, the same as the Norse THOR.

Doris: one of the OCEANIDS, daughter of OCEANUS and
TETHYS. By her brother NEREUS, she bore the fifty
NEREIDS, or sea-nymphs.

Dragon: a fabulous creature frequently encountered
in myth, and always a monstrous type of serpent or
lizard, usually endowed with additional phallic
features such as wings and fiery breath. The dragon
frequently either guards a great treasure or men-
aces a beautiful maiden, and is subdued or slain
by the young god and/or hero, e.g. ZEUS, APOLLO,
PERSEUS.

Dryads: the Greek NYMPHS who inhabit groves and
forests.

Duamutef: in ancient Egypt, one of the four "Sons of
Horus," represented as jackal-headed, who guarded the CANOPIC JAR containing the embalmed
stomach of the deceased.

Duat: one of the ancient Egyptian names for the
afterworld, which in later times was considered
to be beneath the earth, and through which the
sun passes by night on its return journey from west
to east.

Durga, Durgha: in Hindu myth, the terrible aspect,
along with KALI, of PARVATI, consort of SHIVA. See
KALI.

Dwarfs: in Norse myth, the uncanny artificers and craftsmen who are adept in the mining and working of metals and who fashion the marvelous magic weapons and treasures of the gods.

Dyaush-Pitir: very early Hindu sky-god, the name possibly meaning "sky-father."

Dylan: in ancient Welsh myth, a god of the waves and waters of the sea.

E

Ea or Enki: ancient Sumero-Babylonian god of the waters upon the earth, and regarded as the source of wisdom and magic, and as the friend and instructor of mankind in all the arts of civilization. It was Ea who revealed ENLIL's design of destroying mankind by a flood to UTNAPISHTIM, the "Babylonian Noah." His consort is DAMKINA, and their son is MARDUK. Ea together with ANU and Enlil make up the great triad of the most powerful gods.

Eastre or Ostara: ancient Saxon goddess of spring, associated with the fertility of the earth, from whose name and rites the festival of *Easter* is derived.

Ebisu: Japanese god of labor and fishing, son of DAIKOKU.

Echidna: daughter of CETO, with the head of a beautiful nymph and the body of a serpent. By TYPHON she became the mother of, among other monsters, CERBERUS, the Lernean HYDRA, the CHIMAERA and the SPHINX.

Echo: Greek nymph whose duty it was to beguile HERA's attention by incessantly talking to her while ZEUS pursued his amours. Hera discovered the ruse, and punished Echo by causing her always to repeat the voice of another. Her love for the beautiful NARCISSUS was not returned and she pined away till nothing remained but her voice.

Edda: the name of the old Icelandic collections of texts which are our sources for Norse mythology. The oldest is the Elder, or Poetic, Edda, which was later followed by the Younger, or Prose, Edda.

Egeria: in ancient Roman myth, one of the CAMENAE or nymphs, who inspired and guided NUMA, the successor of ROMULUS in the kingship of Rome. Numa used to meet her in a sacred grove in the midst of which a spring gushed forth, and there she taught him wise legislation and the forms of public worship.

Eileithyia: ancient Greek goddess who aided women in labor and presided over childbirth. She became identified with HERA and ARTEMIS, and among the Romans with JUNO as JUNO LUCINA.

Eir: *lit.* "mercy," a Norse goddess of healing.

Eirene: "peace," one of the three HORAE, and daughter of ZEUS and THEMIS.

El: Hebrew dialectic pronunciation of the Semitic IL, meaning "god" in general. The Canaanites of ancient Syria and Palestine called the primordial father-god IL, which see.

Elagabalus: ancient Syrian god, from the Semitic *El Gabal,* "the god of the city of Gabal (Byblos)," on the Phoenician coast, who was associated with the sun, and thus sometimes referred to as HELIOGABALUS. The Roman emperor commonly known by that name assumed it when he was made priest of the god.

Electra: daughter of AGAMEMNON and CLYTEMNESTRA, and sister of IPHGENIA and ORESTES. After the murder of Agamemnon by Clytemnestra and her paramour AEGISTHUS, she saved the life of Orestes and when he grew up incited him to avenge their father's murder and assisted him in the slaying. Orestes later gave her as wife to his friend Pylades.

Eleutherios: "the liberator," an epithet of EROS and DIONYSUS.

Elli: personified Norse goddess of old age, who overcame THOR in wrestling.

Elves: see ALFAR

Elysium, Elysian Fields: In Homer, Elysium forms no part of the realms of HADES and the dead, but is a fabulous and happy land at the western extremities of the earth, inhabited by a few favorites of ZEUS, such as MENELAOS, and RHADAMANTHUS who is its ruler. Later (in Pindar), Elysium becomes the abode of those who have lived three blameless lives. In Hellenistic times it became that part of the underworld where those shades reside who have been adjudged to have led good lives upon earth.

Embla: in Norse myth, the first woman and wife of

ASK the first man, both created from trees and serving as the progenitors of the human race.

Emma-O: Japanese Buddhist lord of the nether world and judge of the dead.

Empusa (Empousa): ancient Greek monstous specter, or vampire, who frightened or devoured travelers.

Enceladus: one of the hundred-armed GIANTS, son of TARTARUS and GAIA, who fought against the Olympians. ZEUS killed him and buried him beneath Mt. Aetna.

Endymion: a beautiful shepherd boy of Asia Minor, beloved of the moon-goddess SELENE, who put him into a deep sleep so that she might be able to embrace him continually.

Enki: see EA

Enkidu: in ancient Mesopotamian myth, the wild creature, half man and half bull, who was created to distract GILGAMESH from his tyrannizing over the people of Uruk. Enkidu was the equal of Gilgamesh in strength, and after an heroic struggle with each other, the two became fast friends. Enkidu was later slain by ISHTAR in revenge upon Gilgamesh, who had refused her love.

Enlil (Ellil): ancient Sumero-Babylonian god of the air, wind and storms, sometimes regarded as the son of ANU. He is sometimes friendly to mankind and sometimes hostile, as when he brought about the great Flood. He holds possession of the "Tablets of Destiny" which give him power over all things. His consort is the goddess NINLIL. Together with Anu and ENKI (or EA), he makes up the great triad of the most powerful gods.

Ennead: the group of the nine chief deities of the Osirian cycle in ancient Egyptian myth: RA-ATUM-KHEPRI, SHU, TEFNUT, GEB, NUT, OSIRIS, ISIS, SET and NEPHTHYS. However, in Egyptian texts the term is frequently used to denote the divine council of gods and goddesses in general.

En-Soph: in Hebrew, *lit.* "the boundless, or infinite one," the term used to designate the primal form of the supreme deity in the KABBALAH, according to which he cannot be perceived by limited human means, and can be described only in terms of what he is not.

Enyo: among the GRAIAE, a minor Greek goddess of war and waster of cities, and a member of the entourage of ARES.

Eos: Greek goddess of the dawn, daughter of HYPERION and sister of HELIOS (the Sun) and SELENE (the Moon). As night draws to a close, she rises from the couch of her spouse TITHONUS and ascends in a chariot drawn by swift horses from the river Oceanus, which encircles the world, to herald the coming light of the sun. The Romans called her AURORA.

Epaphus: son of ZEUS and IO, who bore him when she arrived at the banks of the Nile after her wanderings and recovered her human form. He became king of Egypt and founded the city of Memphis.

Ephialtes: one of the two giant ALOIDAE, who attempted to scale the heavens and dethrone ZEUS.

Epimetheus: son of the TITAN IAPETUS and CLYMENE, and brother of ATLAS and PROMETHEUS. His only claim to fame is that he accepted PANDORA as his wife despite PROMETHEUS's warning to beware of any gifts from ZEUS, and thereby brought ills and sorrows to the world.

Epona: goddess of horses in ancient Gaul, whose cult was adopted by the Roman army.

Erato: Greek Muse of erotic poetry and the mime, normally represented with the lyre. See MUSES.

Erebus: personification of the primeval darkness in the ancient Greek cosmology, born together with NOX (Night) from the primordial CHAOS. In a later period, Erebus was the dark region beneath the earth through which the shades must pass to the realms of HADES below, and is often used metaphorically for Hades itself.

Erechtheus: one of the legendary founders and/or first kings of Athens. His father was HEPHAESTUS, and he was born as a result of the craftsman-god's attempt to rape the goddess ATHENA. Athena put up a powerful resistance, and during the struggle Hephaestus's semen fell upon the Earth, GAIA, and she thus engendered the child Erechtheus, who, as "earth-born," was half man and half serpent. Athena nurtured the child secretly and then put him into a chest which she entrusted to the three daughters of CECROPS, forbidding them to open it. They disobeyed and opened the chest, and when they saw the monstrous form of the child they went mad and threw themselves down from the Acropolis. Erechtheus became king of Athens, and introduced the Panathenaic festival and the four-horsed chariot. In some traditions, he is called ERICHTHONIUS.

Ereshkigal: ancient Sumero-Babylonian goddess who rules over the nether world. She is dark and violent, and by her command ISHTAR is stripped and hung when she descends to her domains in quest of TAMMUZ, and released only when Ereshkigal is tricked into doing so by EA. As ruler over the shades, she receives the mortuary offerings made to the dead.

Erichthonius: one of the legendary founders and/or first king of Athens, and frequently called ERECHTHEUS, which see.

Erinyes: an ancient Greek name for the FURIES.

Eris: Greek goddess of discord and strife, considered to be the sister of ARES and member of his entourage in battle. It was Eris who threw the "Apple of Discord" into the midst of the assembled guests at the wedding of PELEUS and THETIS, which act ultimately brought about the Trojan War.

Eros: Greek god of love and sexual desire. According to an ancient source he was one of the first deities to emerge from primeval CHAOS and hence the oldest of the gods, the power which strives to unite the elements of the Cosmos into harmony. According to the later and more common tradition, he is one of the younger deities, represented as a beautiful nude youth or boy, son of APHRODITE by ZEUS, ARES or HERMES. He flies about on wings, capriciously wounding both gods and men with his unerring and irrestible arrows of desire. In the Orphic theology of the Dionysian Mysteries, Eros is again a most ancient deity and referred to as PROTOGONOS, "the firstborn," having emerged from the cosmic egg of NOX, goddess of night. Sometimes he is accorded a brother, ANTEROS, "return- or opposite-love," who either struggles against love or punishes those do who not return the love of others.

Erytheia: one of the HESPERIDES.

Eshmun: ancient Phoenician version of BAAL.

Esus, Hesus: Latin name for a war-god of the ancient Gauls, whom the Romans identified with MARS.

Eumenides: "The well-minded, or well-disposed ones," a euphemistic Greek term for the FURIES.

Eunomia: *lit.* "good order," one of the three HORAE, and daughter of ZEUS and THEMIS.

Euphrosyne: *lit.* "joy," one of the three GRACES, or CHARITES.

Europa: daughter of Agenor, king of Tyre in Phoenicia, and sister of CADMUS'. She was loved by ZEUS who assumed the form of a beautiful white bull and came forth from the waves as Europa and her maidens were sporting on the shore. Europa, beguiled by the charms of the bull, jumped upon his back, whereupon he rushed back into the sea and swam with her to Crete. There she became, by Zeus, the mother of MINOS, RHADAMANTHUS and SARPEDON.

Eurus: Greek god of the East Wind, son of the TITAN Astraeus and EOS, and brother of BOREAS, ZEPHYRUS and NOTUS. In Latin, VULTURNUS.

Euryale: one of the three GORGONS.

Eurydice: wife of ORPHEUS, killed by a serpent's bite on her wedding day while fleeing from one of her suitors. Inconsolable, Orpheus descended into the realms of HADES in search of her, and by his enchanting music succeeded in charming the rulers of the shades into permitting him to lead Eurydice back to the world of mortals, on condition that he should not look back upon her until they had reached the upper regions. Orpheus, however, was unable to resist looking back, and Eurydice fell back forever among the shades.

Eurynome: an OCEANID, one of the daughters of OCEANUS.

Euterpe: Greek Muse of lyric poetry and music, usually represented with a flute. See MUSES.

F

Fafnir: in Norse myth, obtained the treasure of the DWARFS by violence and guarded it, having changed himself into a venomous serpent. He was killed by SIGURD.

Fama: *lit.* "rumor," whose personified goddess she was among the Romans. What she heard she repeated first in a whisper to a few, then louder and louder until she communicated it to all heaven and earth.

Fates: the three Greek goddesses of human destiny: CLOTHO, the Spinner of the thread of life, LACHESIS, the Disposer, who determines its length and course, and ATROPOS, the Inflexible, who cuts it off.

Fauna: ancient Roman earth-mother and fertility-goddess, usually termed the BONA DEA, and considered the wife, sister and/or daughter of FAUNUS. She was identified with TERRA, TELLUS or OPS.

Faunus: ancient Roman deity of wild nature and fertility, and also regarded as a giver of oracles. He was later identified with PAN. In the plural, the Fauns were analogous to the Greek SATYRS.

Favonius: Latin name for the Greek ZEPHYRUS, the West Wind of spring.

Fenris, Fenrir: in Norse myth, a ravenous wolf, offspring of LOKI. He was bound by a magic chain made of the cat's footfall, the woman's beard, the fish's breath, the bird's spittle, etc., which is the reason these do not exist. At the end of the world he will be released and will fight against the gods, but will be slain.

Fergus: in Celtic myth, a king and hero, one of the warlike lovers of MEDB. His name means "virility," and he is also referred to as "the great horse." Many phallic marvels are ascribed to him.

Fides: *lit.* "faith," personified Roman goddess of good faith and faithfulness.

Flora: Roman goddess, personification of blossoming flowers of spring, and identified with the Greek CHLORIS.

Fomorians: in Celtic myth, one of the mythical prehistoric peoples of Ireland, and regarded as powerful and cruel demons who continually fight against the gods.

Fornax: *lit.* "oven," personified Roman goddess of the baking of bread.

Fortuna: ancient Italian goddess, originally of fertility, and hence of good fortune. She was later identified by the Romans with the Greek TYCHE.

Fravashis: in Zoroastrian myth, the spirits of those humans who are to be created, and guardian spirits of the departed ancestors.

Frey: ruler over the elves, or ALVAR, in ALFHEIM, brother of FRIGGA (FREYA), and husband of GERDA.

Frey, Freyr: in Norse myth, son of NJORD and brother of FREYA. He is a handsome and brave deity who governs good weather and prosperity, joy and peace.

Freya: in Norse myth, daughter of NJORD and sister of FREY, and goddess of love and beauty. She is represented as riding in a chariot drawn by two cats.

Frigg: in Norse myth, the wife of ODIN, mother of BALDER and foremost of the goddesses, probably another aspect of the fertility-goddess FREYA.

Fudo: Japanese Buddhist god of fire and wisdom.

Furies: the avenging goddesses of guilt brought about by murder, perjury and violation of filial piety and the laws of hospitality, pursuing and maddening the perpetrators of these crimes. Their names are ALECTO, "the uneasy," TISIPHONE, "the blood-avenger," and MEGAERA, "the denier," and they sprang from the blood of OURANOS and the Earth (GAIA) upon which it fell, when Ouranos was castrated by his son KRONOS. They are represented as winged maidens with serpents in their hair and blood dripping from their eyes. In Greek they were called ERINYES, and by euphemism the EUMENIDES, "the well-disposed ones."

G

Gad: *lit.* "good fortune" in the Semitic dialect of ancient Syria and Palestine—the protective deity of the ancient Phoenician cities.

Gaea: see GAIA

Gaia (Gaea, Ge): Greek goddess personifying the Earth. She sprang from primeval CHAOS, and in turn bore from herself OURANOS, Sky. Mating with Ouranos, she bore the TITANS, the CYCLOPES and the HEKATONCHEIRES, or hundred-armed GIANTS. In resentment against Ouranos, she incited her sons the Titans to revolt against him. KRONOS, the youngest of the Titans, assumed the leadership, and castrated his father Ouranos.

Galatea: one of the NEREIDS, and the beloved of ACIS. She was also loved by the CYCLOPS POLYPHEMUS, who killed Acis in jealousy.

Galli: the hierodules or priests of CYBELE, who castrated themselves in identification with the goddess.

Gandharvas: in Hindu myth, the celestial singers in the heaven of INDRA, and usually associated with the APSARAS, their feminine counterparts.

Ganesa, Ganesha: in Hindu myth, the son of SHIVA and PARVATI. He is represented as elephant-headed, and is god of wisdom and patron of literature.

Ganga: in Hindu myth, the personified goddess of

the river Ganges, held sacred as flowing from the toe of VISHNU.

Ganymede or **Ganymedes:** legendary Trojan prince, and a boy of remarkable beauty. He was beloved of ZEUS, who assumed the form of an eagle and carried him off to Olympus to be the cupbearer of the gods.

Gautama: see BUDDHA

Ge: see GAIA

Geb: ancient Egyptian personified god of the Earth, son of SHU and TEFNUT, and with his sister and consort NUT (Sky), father of OSIRIS, ISIS, SET and NEPHTHYS.

Gehenna: a corruption of the Hebrew *Ge-ben-Hinnom,* "the valley of the son of Hinnom," originally a place outside Jerusalem where the Canaanites performed human sacrifices and which in later Israelite times became a refuse heap. Because of its unsavory nature and associations, the name came to be used allegorically for the place of punishment of the wicked in the afterlife and synonymous with Hell.

Gemini: *lit.* "the Twins," the brothers CASTOR and POLLUX (the DIOSCURI) placed in the heavens as a constellation.

Genius: one of a class of protective spirits (DAEMONS), guardians of men and of justice. They were later believed to be assigned to men at birth as tutelary deities, accompanying them through life. Among the Romans, every man was believed to have his own Genius whom he worshipped alone with his LARES and PENATES, and every place had its Genius as well. The Genius of womanhood was JUNO.

Gerd, Gerda: in Norse myth, a beautiful giantess, wife of FREY.

Geryon: a triple-bodied, winged giant who dwelt on an island in the extreme west, who had a herd of red cattle guarded by the two-headed dog Orthrus. HERACLES carried off these cattle as one of his Twelve Labors, and killed Geryon.

Ghuls, Ghouls: in pre-Islamic Arab myth, a group of cannibal female JINN who beset lone travelers in the desert, sometimes beguiling them by prostituting themselves to them, and then devouring them.

Giants (Gigantes): they sprang from the blood of the castrated OURANOS which fell upon the Earth (GAIA). They attacked the heavens, but were destroyed by the gods and were buried under Mt. Aetna.

Gigantes: the GIANTS.

Gilgamesh: legendary semidivine epic hero of ancient Mesopotamia, the king of the early Sumerian city of Uruk. Because he ruled tyrannically, the gods created the wild bull-man ENKIDU to distract him, and after a titanic struggle between the two, they became fast friends and went forth to slay the fire-breathing forest ogre *Humbaba* (or *Huwawa*). When ISHTAR offered Gilgamesh her love, he refused, reminding her of the miserable ends of all her former lovers. The furious goddess then sent the Bull of Heaven to destroy Gilgamesh, but he slew it with the aid of Enkidu. In revenge, Ishtar brought about Enkidu's death. After lamenting his friend, Gilgamesh, in quest of the means of avoiding death, set out in quest of his ancestor UTNAPISH-TIM, the "Babylonian Noah," who had survived the Flood and was granted immortality. Utnapish-tim told him the story of the Flood, and told him of a magic plant which could restore youth. Gilgamesh obtained the plant, but it was stolen from him by a serpent, and so Gilgamesh was compelled to suffer the fate of all mortals.

Gilgamesh Epic: ancient Mesopotamian poem, first discovered during the excavations at Nineveh, the capital of the Assyrian kings, in the library collected by King Ashurbanipal. It is inscribed in cuneiform characters on twelve tablets, parts of which were broken and missing. Most of the missing portions have been supplied by fragments discovered in subsequent excavations. It deals with the exploits of GILGAMESH, legendary semidivine king of Uruk, one of the ancient Sumerian cities. On the eleventh tablet is the story of a flood with many striking parallels to the Flood story in the Book of Genesis in the Bible.

Gladsheim: *lit.* "the glad home," in Norse myth the palace of ODIN in ASGARD.

Goblins: in medieval European folklore, mischievous spirits who dwell within hills and caves.

God: in general, a supernatural, immortal being, in his or her attributes a (usually unconscious) projection of the fulfillment of human desires and/or aspirations, and hence conceived of as dominating nature and the cosmos or some aspect thereof, and therefore to be propitiated by mortals.

Golden Fleece: the fleece of the golden ram, the gift of HERMES, upon which PHRIXUS and HELLE flew to escape the wrath of their stepmother INO. When Phrixus arrived at Colchis, he gave the ram to king AEETES, who sacrificed it to ZEUS, and hung its golden fleece on an oak tree in a sacred grove, where it was guarded by a dragon. JASON later carried away the fleece, with the help of MEDEA.

Gorgons: the three frightful sisters, STHENNO, EURY-ALE and MEDUSA, daughters of the sea-monster deities PHORCYS and CETO, and hence sometimes called the PHORCYDES. Their heads were covered with serpents instead of hair, and they had huge fangs and claws. The first two of the Gorgons were immortal, while the third and most famous, Medusa, was mortal, and so terrible was her aspect that whoever looked upon her was turned to stone.

Govannon: in Celtic Welsh myth, the smith of the gods.

Graces: Greek goddesses, personifications of charm and beauty in nature and in human life, and with the MUSES serve as sources of inspiration in poetry and the arts. Their names are EUPHROSYNE ("joy"), THALIA ("bloom") and AGLAIA ("brilliance").

Graiae: the three "old women," or "gray ones," daughters of PHORCYS and CETO, and sisters of the GORGONS. They were gray-haired from birth, and had only one eye and one tooth among them, which they would share. They were named ENYO ("horror"), DEINO ("dread") and PEMPHREDO, ("alarm"). Enyo was sometimes considered as a war goddess who accompanied ARES in battle.

Gratiae: Latin word for the GRACES.

Great Mother: i.e., of the gods, a frequent appellation of CYBELE.

Griffin (Griffon, Gryphon): fabulous animal found in Classical art, one of the forms (like the SPHINX) imported from the East. It had the head and wings of an eagle on the body of a lion, and was believed to guard the gold of the HYPERBOREANS, the dwellers in the unknown regions of the north.

Grimhild, Kriemhild: in Norse myth, a queen who by her sorcery compels SIGURD to marry her daughter GUDRUN.

Gula: one of the ancient Mesopotamian goddesses associated with the underworld.

Gunnar: in Norse myth, a brother of GRIMHILD, the wife of SIGURD. With his brother HOGNI he plotted Sigurd's death.

Gyges: one of the HEKATONCHEIRES, the hundred-armed GIANTS.

H

Hadad (or Adad): ancient Sumero-Babylonian storm-god, whose cult was spread through Asia Minor, where he was also known as TESHUB by the Hittites, and in Syria and Palestine, where he was also known as RESHEF and RIMMON, and represented holding the lightning bolt and wielding a battle mace. Together with SIN and SHAMASH, he makes up the second great triad of Mesopotamian gods.

Hagen: see HOGNI

Haimavati: in Hindu myth, an appellation of DEVI as born of the Himalaya mountains.

Hak: see HEKET

Hades: also called Aides and Aidoneus. Son of KRONOS and brother of ZEUS and POSEIDON, he was allotted the rule of the nether world, which is referred to as the *domain of Hades* or, by transference, as *Hades* alone. Hades has dominion not only over the shades of the dead, but also over all else that is within the earth, namely precious stones and metals. As such he is also termed PLOUTOS, "wealth," and was called by the Romans PLUTO and also DIS. The consort of Hades is PERSEPHONE, (Latin PROSERPINA) daughter of DEMETER, whom he had abducted. Mortals who once enter his domain have no hope of return to the world above, and so Hades is characterized as pitiless and inexorable. Black sheep were offered to him, and the sacrifice was performed with face averted.

In Homer and in the Classic Age, Hades was the abode of all the dead—good and bad alike—much like the SHEOL of the Old Testament. TARTARUS, in the lowest depths of the earth, was the place of eternal punishment of those lesser deities who had committed heinous offenses against the great gods. In the later, post-Classical period, the concept of rewards and punishments for deceased mortals was introduced, with Tartarus as the "Hell" for the wicked and Elysium as the abode of the blessed, but both within the realms of Hades in the underworld. Hence it is a gross innacuracy to translate *Hades* as "Hell."

Halcyone (or Alcyone): in Greek myth, daughter of

AEOLUS and wife of CEYX. When her husband perished in a shipwreck, Halcyone threw herself into the sea. In compassion, the gods changed her and Ceyx into the *halcyon* birds. While the halcyons are breeding, Aeolus restrains his winds and the seas are calm. Hence the halcyon as a symbol of tranquillity and the term "halcyon days."

Hamadryads: the Greek NYMPHS who inhabit trees. Since they are the life-spirit of the tree, they are believed to die when their trees perish.

Hanuman: in Hindu myth, the semidivine Monkey King (or his minister) who aids RAMA in rescuing SITA.

Haoma: in ancient Persian myth, the divine intoxicating juice, the same as the Hindu SOMA, associated with the purification of fire, and believed to have the power of providing husbands for unmarried women.

Hapi, Hapy: ancient Egyptian personified god of the Nile, depicted as a plump man with pendulous female breasts and wearing a headdress of aquatic plants.

Hapy: in ancient Egypt, one of the four "Sons of Horus," represented as ape-headed, who guarded the CANOPIC JAR containing the embalmed lungs of the deceased.

Harmachis: Greek rendering of the ancient Egyptian *Her-Akhety,* "Horus of the Two Horizons," or *Her-em-Akhet,* "Horus upon the Horizon," an epithet of the god HORUS as identified with RA (*Ra Her-Akhety*). The name was sometimes used to refer to the SPHINX of Egypt.

Harmonia: daughter of ARES and APHRODITE, and

wife of CADMUS, founder and king of Thebes. At her marriage, she received from Cadmus a jeweled necklace and a garment, the work of HEPHAESTUS, which proved fatal to those who wished to possess them.

Harpies: "the robbers," demonesses who were believed to have carried off those who disappeared without a trace. Originally represented as fair, winged maidens, they were later described as ugly, noisome birds with maidens' heads. Their names were AËLLO, OCYPETE and CELAENO.

Harpocrates: Greek form of the ancient Egyptian *Her-pa-Khered*, "Horus the Child," the representation of HORUS son of ISIS as a young boy. He is represented in the manner in which children were usually depicted in ancient Egyptian art, nude and holding one finger in his mouth.

Hathor: *lit.* "House of Horus"; ancient Egyptian mother and fertility goddess, sometimes mentioned as mother of RA-HER-AKHETY, "Ra-Horus of the Two Horizons," as his consort and again as his daughter, "the Eye of Ra." As a primeval mother-goddess, she is ambivalent: she is goddess of love, beauty and fertility and represented as a cow, or with cow's horns, is mistress of the afterworld ("Lady of the West"), but is also goddess of slaughter and destruction, delighting in blood; *e.g.* when Ra wished to teach mankind a lesson by killing a large portion of humanity, he called upon Hathor to perform the task, but was able to prevent her from slaughtering all the people on earth only by getting her drunk.

Hebe: personified Greek goddess of the blossoming maturity of youth, and daughter of ZEUS and HERA.

She was the cupbearer of the gods before Zeus bore GANYMEDE up to Olympus. She was called JUVENTAS, "youth," by the Romans, who believed that she had the power to renew the youth of the aged.

Hecate: ancient, pre-Olympian Greek earth-goddess of fertility and magical power, represented by Hesiod as daughter of the PERSES, the TITAN. From Zeus she received a portion of divine power in the realms of heaven, earth and ocean, and presides over good fortune in all aspects of life, and over the bringing of youths to puberty. As earth-goddess, she later became associated with the lower world and night, ghosts and demons, and magic and sorcery, enchanters and sorceresses being her especial protégés.

Hector: eldest son of PRIAM and HECUBA, and the bravest and most chivalrous of the Trojans. He killed PATROCLUS, the friend of ACHILLES, in battle, and thus Achilles was roused out of his withdrawal from the fighting occasioned by his feud with AGAMEMNON. Achilles later killed Hector and kept his body, to prevent its receiving proper burial, but later surrendered it to Priam. He was husband of ANDROMACHE and father of ASTYANAX.

Hecuba: wife of PRIAM, king of Troy, and mother of PARIS and HECTOR. After the fall of Troy, she was taken captive by the Achaeans and enslaved.

Heimdal: in Norse myth, a son of ODIN and one of the chief deities of ASGARD and the watchman of the gods, guarding the rainbow-bridge BIFROST against the giants.

Heka: see HEKET

Hekabe: original Greek name of the wife of PRIAM,

king of Troy; better known by her Latin name
HECUBA.

Hekatoncheires: the three hundred-armed GIANTS,
sons of OURANOS and GAIA: BRIAREUS, COTTUS and
GYGES. They later aided the Olympians in their
war with the TITANS.

Heket (Heka): ancient Egyptian frog-headed goddess, regarded as the consort of KHNEMU (KHNUM)
and associated with creation and birth. The frog,
presumably because of the millions of them
spawned after the annual inundation of the Nile,
was regarded as a symbol of fertility and great
multiplication.

Hel, Hell: in Norse myth, the daughter of LOKI and
the giantess ANGERBODA, described as a horrible
hag and ruler over the realms of the dead, which
are also called by her name, in the darkest and
coldest regions of NIFLHEIM, beneath the roots of
YGGDRASIL.

Helen: daughter of TYNDAREUS and LEDA, or according to a more popular tradition, of Leda and
ZEUS, who visited her in the form of a swan, and
sister of CASTOR, POLLUX and CLYTEMNESTRA. She
was considered the most beautiful woman in the
world, and in her youth was abducted by THESEUS,
but was rescued by her brothers Castor and Pollux
during Theseus's absence in Hades. She later became the wife of MENELAOS, king of Sparta, and was
subsequently carried off to Troy by Paris. This act
brought about the Trojan War.

Heliogabalus: see ELAGABALUS

Helios: the Greek god of the sun (the Roman SOL),
son of HYPERION and brother of SELENE (the Moon)

and EOS (the Dawn). By Perse, the OCEANID, he became the father of AEËTES, CIRCE and PASIPHAE.

Helle: daughter of ATHAMAS and NEPHELE and sister of PHRIXUS. She and her brother escaped from the wrath of their stepmother INO on the back of the ram with the GOLDEN FLEECE, the gift of HERMES. Helle fell into the sea, which was named the *Hellespont* after her.

Hemera: personification of Day in the ancient Greek cosmogony, born of EREBUS (Darkness) and NOX (Night).

Hephaestus: Greek deity of craftsmanship, metalwork and worker with fire in general, with whom the Romans identified the god VULCAN. According to some authorities, he is the son of ZEUS and HERA; according to others, Hera bore him without any father to spite Zeus in bringing ATHENA forth independently of her. He was born lame and weak, and his mother disliked him so intensely that she threw him down from Olympus. He became the great smith and artificer of the gods, being associated from ancient times with volcanic fire (hence the word *volcano*, from his Roman name), and is assisted by the CYCLOPES. Ironically, he was given the goddess APHRODITE as his lawful spouse. Her many amours and her infidelity to Hephaestus were notorious, and in Homer the gods enjoy a good laugh when Hephaestus, by forging an invisible net with the strength of steel, catches Aphrodite with ARES *in flagrante delicto*.

Hera: queen of the Olympian deities, sister and wife of ZEUS. She was the eldest daughter of KRONOS and RHEA. The poets represented her as constantly jealous of Zeus's various amours and so pursuing her rivals, both among goddesses and mortal women, with implacable fury. She represents the proprieties of the marriage bond and family life, and in her fertility aspect is goddess of childbirth. Her principal sanctuary was at Argos in the Peloponnesus. Her most common emblem is the peacock. Among the Romans she was identified with JUNO.

Heracles: Greek demigod, son of ZEUS and ALCMENE, wife of AMPHITRYON of Thebes. He was famous for his great strength from his very birth, having strangled in his cradle two serpents sent by HERA to destroy him. He is most famous for the Twelve Labors which he had to perform while serving Eurystheus, king of Tiryns. These were: 1) the killing of the monstrous Nemean lion; 2) the slaying of the Lernean HYDRA; 3) the capture of the Arcadian stag; 4) the capture of the Erymanthean boar; 5) the cleansing of the Augean stables; 6) the destruction of the Stymphalian birds; 7) the capture of the Cretan bull; 8) the capture of the man-eating mares of Diomedes; 9) the procuring of the girdle of HIPPOLYTE, queen of the AMAZONS; 10) the capture of the oxen of GERYON; 11) the fetching of the golden apples of the HESPERIDES; 12) and the most difficult, the bringing up of CERBERUS from Hades.

Hercules: Latin form of the Greek HERACLES.

Hermaphroditus: son of HERMES and APHRODITE. Possessing the outstanding beauty of both his parents, he was loved by the NYMPH who resided in the spring of SALMACIS. She declared her love while he was bathing in her spring, but he rejected her. Thereupon she prayed to the gods that she might be united with him forever. Her request was granted, and "they became one flesh," a being with the physical characteristics of both sexes. Hence arose the legend that any man who bathed in the spring Salmacis would become effeminate. The tradition of the androgynous deity was common in the ancient East, reflecting a basic bisexuality of the human psyche, and later rationalized into a symbol of the generation of the universe.

Hermensul: see IRMINSUL

Hermes: Greek god of trade, riches and good fortune, also the messenger or herald of the gods, and as *Psychopompos*, the conductor of the shades of the dead into Hades. Also, because of the exploits ascribed to him, he was the patron deity of tricksters and thieves. He was an early fertility deity, and crude phallic images of him called *hermae* were set up at crossroads and in front of houses. Hermes was the son of ZEUS and MAIA, daughter of ATLAS, who was one of the TITANS. He is represented wearing the *petasos*, or broad-brimmed traveler's hat, and winged sandals. He usually carries the herald's staff *(caduceus)*, intertwined with ribbons or serpents. His Roman name was MERCURY.

Hermes Trismegistus: *lit.* "thrice-greatest Hermes," an identification, in late Classical times, of the Greek HERMES with the ancient Egyptian THOTH. The god Thoth, in Egypt, was the scribe of the gods and the inventor of the art of writing, and as such was the patron deity of knowledge and the sciences in general, of which magic constituted an important part. The Greeks considered the Egyptians to be the repository of all secret wisdom, believed to be embodied in certain esoteric books written by Thoth, "the thrice-greatest Hermes," and referred to as the *Hermetic Writings*.

Hermione: daughter of MENELAOS and HELEN. She was later married to ORESTES.

Hertha: see NERTHUS

Hesperia: one of the HESPERIDES.

Hesperides: the "daughters of Evening," the goddesses who guarded the golden apples given by GAIA to HERA at her marriage to ZEUS. They live at the western extreme of the Mediterranean, near Mt. Atlas, hence they are sometimes considered daughters of ATLAS. Their names are AEGLE, ARETHUSA, ERYTHEIA and HESPERIA.

Hesperis: *lit.* "evening," personified as a Greek goddess, wife of ATLAS and mother of the HESPERIDES.

Hesperus: the evening star, son of EOS.

Hestia (Latin VESTA) : daughter of KRONOS and RHEA, and goddess of the hearth fire, hence presiding over domestic life. She was also the particular goddess over the altar fires in the temples. She was a virgin-goddess, and when wooed by POSEIDON and APOLLO, swore by the head of ZEUS to remain a virgin. The Romans called her VESTA, and her round temple stood in the Forum. There was no statue of the goddess there, but she was identified with the eternal fire which had to be kept burning on her altar. See VESTALS.

Hesus: see ESUS

Hippogriff: fabulous animal represented in ancient Greek art, half horse and half GRIFFIN.

Hippolyte: daughter of ARES, queen of the AMAZONS and sister of ANTIOPE. One of the twelve labors of HERACLES was to fetch the girdle of Hippolyte, which she had received from her father Ares. She was slain by Heracles in the battle which ensued.

Hippolytus: son of THESEUS by ANTIOPE, queen of the AMAZONS (or by her sister HIPPOLYTE). He lived at the court of Theseus when PHAEDRA was queen. Phaedra fell in love with him, and when he refused her advances, she hanged herself, accusing Hippolytus of having seduced her. Theseus thereupon called down upon him the curse of his father POSEIDON, who sent a bull from the sea to frighten the horses of Hippolytus's chariot. It overturned, and Hippolytus was dragged to his death.

Hippomenes: Greek youth, descendant of POSEIDON who loved ATALANTA, and won her by conquering her in the foot race to which she challenged her suitors, by means of the three golden apples given him by APHRODITE. He dropped them one at a time, and Atalanta stopped to pick up each one, thus allowing him to win the race.

Hoenir: in Norse myth, one of the ancient gods who with ODIN took part in the creation of man. Hoenir gave man his soul.

Hogni, Hagen: in Norse myth, a brother of GRIMHILD, the wife of SIGURD. With his brother GUNNAR he plotted Sigurd's death.

Holda, Holle: in Teutonic folklore, a fertility goddess connected with the lunar cult, also known as *Dame Holle*.

Holle: see HOLDA

Horae (the Hours): Greek goddesses regulating the seasons, guardians of the order of nature in general and of the gates of Olympus. They were the daughters of ZEUS and THEMIS, and are named EUNOMIA ("good order"), DIKE ("justice") and EIRENE ("peace"), indicating the concept of human morality as part of the natural order of the cosmos.

Horus: one of the principal deities of ancient Egypt, represented as a hawk or falcon, or in human form with a falcon's head, often crowned with the sun-disc encircled by the *uraeus*-serpent. There were two main concepts of Horus:

a) The solar Horus, identified with RA and called *Her-Akhety*, "Horus of the Two Horizons," or *Ra-Her-Akhety*, or *Horus the Elder*.

b) Horus the son of ISIS and OSIRIS, who avenged his father, who had been slain by SET, and came into his rightful possession of the throne. The living king of Egypt was always regarded as Horus incarnate. Horus is often depicted as a child (*Her-pa-Khered*, "Horus the Child," rendered as HARPOCRATES by the Greeks), and as such is shown nude, with the child's side lock and his finger in his mouth, wearing the double crown of Egypt, and often being suckled by Isis or HATHOR. See OSIRIS.

Hotei: Japanese god of happiness and laughter, depicted as very fat, and carrying a huge linen bag of treasures on his back.

Houris: in Islam, the beautiful celestial damsels who will be awarded to the faithful in heaven.

Hours: see HORAE

How-Too: ancient Chinese earth-god depicted as a monster and dwelling within mountains and rivers.

Huixtocihuatl: Aztec or pre-Aztec fertility-goddess, connected particularly with salt and salt water.

Hurakan: ancient Mayan god of wind and storm who visited the anger of the gods upon mankind by bringing about the Flood. The word *hurricane* comes from his name.

Hyacinthus: a beautiful youth beloved of both APOLLO and ZEPHYRUS. He returned the love of Apollo and not of Zephyrus. As he and Apollo were throwing the discus together, the jealous Zephyrus blew Apollo's discus out of its course, causing it to strike the head of Hyacinthus and kill him. From his blood Apollo made spring up the flower bearing the name of Hyacinthus.

Hyades: *lit.* "the rainy ones," seven nymphs, daughters of ATLAS and sisters of the PLEIADES, and regarded as the nurses either of the infant ZEUS or the infant DIONYSUS, in reward for which they were placed as a constellation in the heavens. Rainy weather began when they rose with the sun in May.

Hydra: a legendary seven-headed, fire-breathing dragon, offspring of TYPHON and ECHIDNA, who ravaged the Lernean swamps in Argos, and was slain by HERACLES.

Hygieia: personified Greek goddess of health, regarded as the daughter of AESCULAPIUS. She is represented as a maiden with a serpent, to whom she gives drink from a cup in her hand.

Hymen or **Hymenaeus:** ancient Greek god of marriage (actually a personification of the *marriage song*), represented as a handsome youth, son of APOLLO and one of the MUSES.

Hyperboreans: in Greek myth, a legendary people believed to live "beyond the north wind," in a land of unbroken sunshine, where they enjoyed continuous happiness.

Hyperion: one of the TITANS, son of OURANOS and GAIA, and father of HELIOS, SELENE and EOS.

Hypermnestra: the only one of the DANAIDES who spared her husband LYNCEUS, and became by him ancestress of the kings of the Argives.

Hypnos: personified Greek god of sleep, and the son of NOX.

I

Iacchus: the name by which DIONYSUS was hailed in the Eleusinian Mysteries, sometimes equated with BACCHUS, although at Eleusis Dionysus was regarded as the son of ZEUS and DEMETER.

Iapetus: one of the TITANS. By CLYMENE, daughter of OCEANUS and TETHYS, he became the father of ATLAS, PROMETHEUS and EPIMETHEUS.

Iasion (Iasius, Iasus): son of ZEUS and the OCEANID Electra. He was loved by DEMETER, who bore him BOÖTES and PLUTUS. In jealousy, Zeus slew him with his thunderbolt.

Ibis: a cranelike bird of ancient Egypt with a long,

curved beak. It is the bird of the god THOTH, who is usually represented as ibis-headed, and it was regarded as sacred by the ancient Egyptians.

Iblis: an archdemon in Islamic theology, and often equated with the DEVIL.

Icarius: legendary Athenian who welcomed DIONYSUS to Attica and in return received the gift of the vine from the god. Icarius gave wine to the shepherds, and when they became intoxicated they thought that he had poisoned them, and so slew him. His daughter Erigone found his body, to which she was led by his faithful dog Maera, and hanged herself in grief. Dionysus punished the land by a plague, and infected the maidens with madness so that they hanged themselves as did Erigone.

Icarus: son of DAEDALUS, who flew out over the Aegaean sea with his father to escape from Crete, flying with the wings which his father had made of feathers and wax. Icarus, however, flew too near the sun, the wax melted, and he fell into the sea and was drowned. In his memory a portion of the Aegaean was named the *Icarian Sea*.

Ichor: the fluid which flowed through the veins of the gods in Classical mythology, corersponding to the blood of mortals.

Idaea: an epithet of CYBELE, referring to her connection with Mt. Ida in Asia Minor, which was an ancient seat of her worship.

Idaean Dactyls: see DACTYLS

Idun: in Norse myth, the consort of BRAGI, god of poetry. She possesses the apples which she gives to the gods to restore their eternal youth.

Igigi: in ancient Mesopotamia, sometimes a term for the gods of heaven, as the ANUNNAKI are the gods of the earth, but in some texts the positions are reversed.

Il or El: in the Semitic languages, *lit.* "God." In ancient Syria and Palestine, the old deity of the Canaanites was called *Il,* i.e. *"the* god, *par excellence"* and was progenitor of the other deities. In most of the texts he is regarded as being old and as having retired in favor of the younger deities, such as BAAL, who is the active fertility principle of the cosmos, and for this reason the later Greek writers equated him with KRONOS. His consort is usually ASHERAH/ASHTART.

Imhotep: *lit.* "He who comes in peace" in ancient Egyptian, the vizier of the Pharaoh Zoser, the first king of the Third Dynasty (about 2700 B.C.). He was also a physician, philosopher, architect and engineer, and was the builder of Zoser's Step Pyramid. He was subsequently deified, and regarded as a patron god of scribes and others of his professions.

Imsu: see MIN

Inachus: personified deity of the river of that name in Greece, the son of OCEANUS and TETHYS, and the father of IO.

Inari: Japanese agricultural deity whose animal is the fox. He is often identified with the fertility goddess UKEMOCHI.

Indra: in Hindu myth, one of the ADITYAS, guardian deities of the months, and god of rain, thunderstorm and battle, often represented riding on an elephant.

Ininna: early Sumerian name of the Mesopotamian fertility and war goddess ISHTAR, which see.

Ino: daughter of CADMUS, king of Thebes, and HARMONIA, and sister of SEMELE and AGAVE. By ATHAMAS, king of Orchomenos, she became the mother of LEARCHUS and MELICERTES, and intrigued against the children of NEPHELE, the first wife of Athamas. Athamas, driven mad, killed Learchus, and Ino threw herself with Melicertes into the sea, where they became marine deities, Ino becoming LEUCOTHEA, the "White Goddess," and Melicertes PALAEMON.

Io: daughter of the river-god INACHUS, first king of Argos. She was loved by ZEUS, who changed her into a heifer in fear of the jealous wrath of HERA. Hera, aware of the metamorphosis, had her pursued and guarded by the hundred-eyed ARGUS, whom Zeus then had HERMES slay. Hera then sent a gadfly to pursue her and drive her into a mad frenzy, and she fled through Asia, swimming across the Ionian Sea and the Bosporus ("cow ford") until she came to Egypt. There she recovered her human form and gave birth to EPAPHUS, her son by Zeus.

Iphigenia (Iphigeneia): daughter of AGAMEMNON and CLYTEMNESTRA. Because Agamemnon had killed a hart sacred to ARTEMIS, the goddess caused the Achaean fleet to be becalmed at Aulis on the way to Troy. To appease Artemis, Agamemnon was commanded to sacrifice Iphigenia to her, after which favorable winds prevailed once more. According to one tradition, Artemis substituted a stag for Iphigenia as she was about to be sacrificed, and spirited her away to Tauris, where she became the priestess of the goddess.

Irene: see EIRENE

Iris: personified Greek goddess of the rainbow, and regarded as the messenger of the gods to mankind.

Irminsul: pagan Teutonic fertility-deity, personified in a pillar called "the Column of the World," which was destroyed by Charlemagne.

Ishtar (or **Innina**): ancient Sumero-Babylonian mother and fertility goddess, and like all the great goddesses of the ancient Near East, also goddess of bloodshed, war and destruction. She absorbed most of the attributes of the other and earlier goddesses, and became known as either the consort or daughter of ANU. She is represented as riding upon the lion, her sacred animal, and is also associated with the dragon. She was worshipped as goddess of love and procreation and also as goddess of war, particularly by the Assyrians. Her most important myth is that in which she is the lover of TAMMUZ, who is either her brother or her son. He is slain, and Ishtar laments him and then descends to the nether world whence after various trials she brings him back in triumph, after which joy and fertility return to the earth.

Isis: ancient Egyptian mother and fertility goddess, daughter of GEB and NUT and sister of OSIRIS, SET and NEPHTHYS. For the story of Isis, Osiris and Set and the birth of HORUS, see OSIRIS. As great fertility-goddess, she is frequently identified with HATHOR, and like the latter is also usually depicted with cow's horns. She is also "Great of Magic" and a powerful sorceress, and when RA grew old she was able to have the ancient god poisoned by a serpent which she made, so that she could force him to reveal to her his secret name, as the price of her healing him.

Ixion: mythical Greek king who sought, and imagined that he obtained, the love of HERA. When he boasted of this exploit, he was hurled down into TARTARUS, where he was bound to an eternally revolving wheel.

Izanagi and **Izanami:** respectively "the male who invites" and "the female who invites," Japanese deities who brought forth the great gods at creation.

J

Jagganath: in Hindu myth, an idol whose name means "lord of the world" and which is believed to contain the bones of KRISHNA. At his festival the image is drawn about in a ponderous cart, beneath whose wheels his devotees used to throw themselves to be crushed to death; the origin of *juggernaut.*

Jahveh: see YAHWEH

Jamshid: in ancient Persian myth a legendary early king who reigned for seven hundred years, introducing the culture of the vine and other useful arts to mankind.

Janus: Roman god of gates and doors and hence represented with a double-faced head, each looking in opposite directions. The month of January was sacred to him. His temple at Rome was kept closed in time of peace and open in time of war. It is said that the temple was closed only three times in Roman history.

Jason: son of AESON, king of Iolcus in Thessaly. Aeson's half brother PELIAS had usurped the throne and attempted to kill Jason, who escaped. When he had grown, Jason returned and demanded the throne, which Pelias promised him if he would journey to Colchis and fetch the GOLDEN FLEECE which was guarded by AEËTES the king. Jason then organized the expedition to Colchis, sailing in the ship *Argo*, and accompanied by the great heroes of Greece. With the assistance of MEDEA, daughter of Aeëtes, he obtained the fleece and returned to Iolcus, where Medea caused the death of Pelias. Jason later deserted Medea, at which she killed her children by him, and Jason died of grief.

Jehovah: the name has been used to designate the Deity as named in the Old Testament. This name is a misreading of the Hebrew text, as found with the vowel points added, and never existed as such. For the correct name, see YAHWEH; also TETRA-GRAMMATON.

Jinn: in Islamic belief, a general term for various species of DEMONS and spirits, including those of the pre-Islamic deities.

Jizo: Japanese god, protective deity of children and consoler of troubled parents.

Jocasta: legendary queen of Thebes, wife of LAIUS and mother and later wife of OEDIPUS. When she discovered her incestuous union with Oedipus, she hanged herself.

Jormungand: in Norse myth, one of the three children of LOKI and ANGERBODA, known as the MIDGARD SERPENT.

Jotunheim: in Norse myth, the home of the JOTUNS, in the snowy regions on the outermost shores of the ocean.

Jotuns: in Norse myth, the primeval frost-giants who were drowned in the blood of YMIR.

Jove: another Latin form of JUPITER.

Juggernaut: see JAGGANATH

Juno: Roman queen of the gods, and identified by them with the Greek HERA. The Romans regarded Juno as the protective spirit of women, symbolizing her sexual powers and activities, and just as each man had his GENIUS, so each woman had her Juno. The attributes of the Greek birth-goddesses EILEITHYIA were assimilated to her, and as such she was entreated by women in labor as Juno LUCINA.

Jupiter: chief god of the Romans, whom they equated with ZEUS.

Juventas: *lit.* "youth" in Latin, the Roman name for the Greek goddess HEBE.

K

Ka: in ancient Egyptian belief, the Divine Essence of gods and men. When a mortal was born, his Ka was created with him and remained in the world of eternity while his mortal body was alive on earth. When a man died, he "rejoined his Ka."

Kabbalah: *lit.* "the received tradition," a collection of works, mostly in Hebrew Aramaic, dating from early medieval times, and purporting to be an interpretation of the Pentateuch in the Bible. It is full of mystic theosophical concepts, related to Neo-platonism and Gnosticism, concerning the nature of the Deity and its relationship to the cosmos and to man. The assumption is that every word and letter has a hidden, mystical meaning which can be learned by the initiate.

Kalchas (Calchas): of Mycenae, and in Homer the greatest of the seers who accompanied the Achaeans on the expedition against Troy. He was defeated by MOPSUS in a contest in the prophetic arts, and died of vexation.

Kali: *lit.* "the black one," in Hindu myth the terrible and destructive aspect of PARVATI, consort of SHIVA. She is draped with severed human heads, and she tramples upon the slain body of her husband in her frenzy.

Kalki: *lit.* "time," in Hindu myth, the tenth and last incarnation of VISHNU, who will come from the sky upon a white horse and wreak final destruction upon the wicked, renew creation and restore righteousness.

Kama: in Hindu myth, the god of love, son of LAKSHMI. He is represented as a winged youth bearing bow and arrows, like the Greek EROS.

Kami: in Japanese myth, the "superior ones," the deified spirits of the deceased ancestors.

Karma: in Buddhism, the accumulated consequences of one's acts, brought about by desire, which turn the wheel of continual expiatory rebirths.

Kartikeya: in Hindu myth, a war-god, son of AGNI or SHIVA. He led the celestial armies of good against the evil demon-king TARAKA.

Keb: see GEB

Kebehsenuf: in ancient Egypt, one of the four "Sons of Horus" represented as falcon-headed, who guarded the CANOPIC JAR containing the embalmed intestines of the deceased.

Kedesh, Kedeshet: *lit.* "the holy one" or "holiness," in ancient Syro-Palestinian myth an epithet of ASHTART. During the cosmopolitan period of New Kingdom Egypt, she is depicted there as a nude goddess, standing on a lion and holding serpents and/or lotus flowers in her outstretched hands.

Ker: usually found in the plural (Keres), ancient Greek goddesses of death and doom who also act as avenging spirits. In later times they were regarded as the vengeful spirits of the dead.

Khepry (Khepri, Khepera): in ancient Egyptian *lit.* "he who comes into being" or "he who brings into being," one of the forms of the primeval Egyptian god RA, associated with the sun, who

came into being by himself out of the primordial waters. Since the Egyptian word *kheper* also
means the scarabaeus-beetle, Ra in this aspect is
frequently represented as a beetle holding the sun-
disc in its foreclaws, or in human form with a
beetle for a head.

Khnemu (Khnum): ancient Egyptian creator-god,
represented as ram-headed, who fashioned the
bodies of both gods and mankind upon his pot-
ter's wheel.

Khnum: see KHNEMU

Khonsu (Khensu): the son of the deities AMEN and
MUT of ancient Egypt, and depicted in human
form, with the child's side lock and the curved
beard worn by the gods. He was also a moon-deity,
and as such often wears the moon and crescent on
his headdress.

Kingu: in ancient Babylonian myth, the second consort of TIAMAT after her first, APSU, had been slain
by EA (ENKI). Tiamat had given Kingu the "Tablets of Destiny," which MARDUK took from him and
fastened on his own breast after he had slain Tiamat. Kingu too was later executed, and from his
blood mankind was created.

Kishi Bojin: Japanese goddess originating in India,
a fertility deity and protectress of young children.

Kobold: in Teutonic folklore a dwarf or earth-spirit
dwelling in mines.

Koran: the body of Islamic scriptures dictated to his
disciples by Mohammed, who stated that they were
revealed to him by the angel Gabriel.

Kore: *lit.* "the maiden," a frequent epithet of the
Greek goddess PERSEPHONE.

Kouretes (Curetes): demigods armed with bronze weapons, associated with the Cretan RHEA. The latter committed the infant ZEUS to their care, in order to hide him from KRONOS. To drown the cries of the divine child, the Kouretes executed a wild war dance, clashing their spears against their shields. They taught the Cretans the arts of agriculture and metalworking. As the orgiastic attendants upon the ancient mother-goddess, they are often associated with the CORYBANTES of the Phrygian RHEA CYBELE.

Kriemhild: see GRIMHILD

Krishna: in Hindu myth, the eighth of the ten incarnations of VISHNU. He is one of the most popular of the gods, and many stories are told of his exploits, his flute playing and dalliance with the legendary milkmaids.

Kronos (Cronus): youngest of the TITANS, sons of OURANOS and GAIA. Ouranos, jealous of his sons, thrust them deep down beneath the earth. Gaia, in resentment at this and because Ouranos had caused her to bear so many children, produced a sickle of steel with which she incited the Titans to castrate their father. None dared do this except Kronos, who stealthily accomplished the deed while Ouranos slept. Thereupon Kronos assumed the rule, later destined in turn to be unseated by his son ZEUS. The reign of Kronos was sometimes regarded as the Golden Age. Mating with his sister RHEA, he became by her the father of the third generation of gods, the deities HESTIA, DEMETER, HERA, HADES, POSEIDON and ZEUS. Kronos too was fearful of his children, and devoured each one immediately at birth. When the youngest child, Zeus, was born, however, Rhea deceived Kronos by presenting him with a stone wrapped in swaddling clothes, which Kronos promptly swallowed. Zeus, who had been hidden, grew to maturity and, overpowering his father, made him disgorge the children whom he had swallowed. With the aid of his brothers, his sisters and his other partisans among the gods, Zeus overpowered and dethroned Kronos and became king of gods and men.

Kuan-Ti: Chinese god of war who, unlike other such deities, is concerned with averting conflict and protecting mankind from its horrors.

Kuan-Yin, Kwan-Yin: ancient Chinese Buddhist mother and fertility goddess, protectress of mankind in general, and personification of pity and mercy.

Kukulkan: ancient Mayan deity, "the feathered serpent" whose attributes were often merged with those of QUETZALCOATL. He is a culture-deity, inventor of the calendar and patron of craftsmen.

Kumara: an appellation of KARTIKEYA, which see.

Kwannon: Japanese name for KUAN-YIN.

Kwan-Yin: see KUAN-YIN

Kwei: Chinese term for the spirits of the dead.

Kypris: an epithet of APHRODITE, as being risen from the sea off the island of Cyprus.

L

Labyrinth: the underground maze artfully contrived for MINOS, king of Crete, by the master craftsman DAEDALUS, and from which no one who entered could find his way out. There Minos confined the MINOTAUR, who found and devoured the human victims forced to enter it.

Lachesis: one of the three FATES. She is the Disposer, who measures off the length of the thread of human life spun by CLOTHO, and determines its destiny.

Ladon: the dragon who guarded the golden apples of the HESPERIDES, and who was slain by HERACLES.

Laius: legendary king of Thebes, husband of JOCASTA and father of OEDIPUS, which see.

Lamia: in Classical myth, a child-stealing demon, usually female but sometimes referred to as male or bisexual. According to some, she stole children because her own, by ZEUS, were destroyed by HERA.

Lakshmi: in Hindu myth, also known as SRI, goddess of good fortune and beauty, and mother of KAMA, the young god of love. She arose from the milky foam of the waves at the "Churning of the Ocean." She is the consort of VISHNU, and is his wife during each of his incarnations.

Laocoön: Trojan priest of APOLLO, who attempted to warn the Trojans of the Achaean trick of the wooden horse. For this, ATHENA, who favored the

Achaeans, caused two monstrous serpents to emerge from the sea and strangle Laocoön and his two sons.

Laomedon: king of Troy and father of PRIAM, TITHONUS and others. POSEIDON and APOLLO, who had incurred the wrath of ZEUS, had to hire themselves out to him, and he made them build the walls of Troy. Afterwards he refused to pay them their wages, and they visited the country with misfortunes. Laomedon was eventually killed by HERACLES.

Lares: the deified ancestral spirits of the Roman family and included among the PENATES, the household gods who were the protective family deities. As progenitors of the family, they were accompanied by symbolic phallic serpents.

Latona: Roman name of LETO.

Laverna: Roman goddess of thieves, impostors, and frauds.

Learchus: son of ATHAMAS and INO. He was slain by Athamas, who was seized with madness when he incurred the wrath of HERA as result of Ino's intrigues against Athamas's children by NEPHELE.

Leda: wife of TYNDAREUS, king of Sparta. She was beloved of ZEUS, who visited her in the form of a swan, with the result that she laid an egg, in which were CASTOR, POLLUX, HELEN and CLYTEMNESTRA. According to one tradition, Leda was embraced by both Zeus and Tyndareus in the same night, and in the egg were Pollux and Helen as children of Zeus, while Castor and Clytemnestra were children of Tyndareus.

Legba: a fetishistic personal god of the Africans of

Dahomey, phallic in nature. Every individual had his *legba*.

Lemures: Roman name for the ghosts of the dead, who were appeased at the annual festival called the *Lemuria*.

Lenaeus: an appellation of DIONYSUS as lord of the wine press.

Lethe: one of the mythical rivers flowing through the realms of HADES. The shades of the dead drank of its waters, thereby obtaining forgetfulness of their past life.

Leto: daughter of the TITANS Coeus and PHOEBE, and mother of APOLLO and ARTEMIS by ZEUS.

Leucothea: in Greek "the White Goddess," the name of INO as marine deity, which she became when she threw herself into the sea with her son MELI-CERTES.

Leviathan: in the Hebrew dialect of the Old Testament, the pronunciation of the Canaanite LOTAN, which see.

Liber: in Latin, *lit.* "the free one," an ancient Italian fertility-god whom the Romans later identified with DIONYSUS. He had a feminine counterpart, *Libera,* whom the Romans identified with PER-SEPHONE.

Lif: *lit.* "life," in Norse myth the woman who will be left alive after RAGNAROK, and with LIFTHRASIR will beget a new race of mankind.

Lifthrasir: *lit.* "he who holds fast to life," in Norse myth the man who will be left alive after RAG-NAROK, and with LIF will beget a new race of mankind.

Liknites: *lit.* "he of the winnowing fan" (a sort of shovel with which the cut grain was thrown into the air to separate the chaff). An epithet of DIONYSUS, alluding to a fertility aspect of the god. The winnowing fan was one of the implements used in the Mysteries.

Lilith: *lit.* "she of the night"; a night-demoness of ancient Assyria, mentioned in the Old Testament and adopted into medieval Judeo-Christian demonology as a sort of LAMIA, and usually regarded as being in the form of a beautiful woman with long, streaming hair, flying about as a night owl and making away with children.

Linga, Lingam: in Hinduism, the male generative organ, or PHALLUS as a concrete symbol, particularly of the god SHIVA in his generative aspects. See YONI.

Linus: an ancient Greek name for the god who is killed and/or torn to pieces, and hence for the dirge or lamentation sung at the ritual commemorating his death. In one version of the myth, Linus is a son of APOLLO by a mortal princess, is reared by shepherds and later torn to pieces by his own dogs. In another version he is killed by his father Apollo for challenging him to a musical contest. In another, Linus taught the use of the lyre to HERACLES, who killed him in a fit of passion when he reprimanded him.

Lodur: in Norse myth, one of the ancient gods who with ODIN took part in the creation of man. Lodur gave man blood and bodily color.

Loki: in Norse myth, one of the major deities. By race a giant and considered one of the AESIR, although actually their enemy. He is handsome, but crafty and malicious. He is also connected with fire and magic, and by the giantess ANGERBODA begot the evil creatures FENRIR, JORMUNGAND and HEL.

Lotan: in ancient Syro-Palestinian myth, a monstrous primeval serpent or dragon who was slain by BAAL. In the Hebrew dialect of the Old Testament, he is referred to as LEVIATHAN.

Lotis: a NYMPH, daughter of POSEIDON. She was pursued by PRIAPUS, and in order to escape him was changed into the lotus tree.

Lucifer: *lit.* "the light-bearer" (Greek *Phosphoros*), the name given to the planet Venus as morning star, and called the son of EOS as a personified deity. In medieval Christian theology the name was applied to the chief of the angels who rebelled and was cast down into Hell, and identified with SATAN.

Lucina: the epithet of JUNO as goddess presiding over childbirth, probably as "she who brings children into the light (Latin: *lux*) ." See EILEITHYIA.

Lucretia (Lucrece): wife of a cousin of TARQUIN, one of the early kings of Rome. Her rape at the hands of one of Tarquin's sons, and her consequent suicide, brought about the fall of the Tarquinian dynasty.

Lug: in Celtic myth, a young and beautiful god with some of the attributes of the Greek APOLLO. He is the "many-skilled," being adept with the spear and the sling, a carpenter and a smith, and also poet, historian, sorcerer and magician.

Luna: Latin word for the moon and name of its personified goddess, equivalent to the Greek SELENE.

Lynceus: son of AEGYPTUS and husband of HYPERM-
NESTRA, the DANAÏD, who spared his life. He succeeded DANAÜS as king of Argos.

M

Maat: ancient Egyptian personified goddess of truth,
equity, justice, the right order of things, etc., represented as wearing her symbol, the ostrich feather,
upon her head. She is sometimes regarded as a
daughter of RA, and is frequently present at the
judgment of the deceased before OSIRIS, where the
heart of the deceased is weighed against the feather
of Truth.

Madb: in Celtic myth the queen of King CONCHOBAR,
and the warlike enemy of CUCHULAINN. She is also
a powerful sorceress, and in all probability was
originally a fighting goddess of the mother/fertility
type. It is believed that she is the origin of the
"Queen Mab" of British folklore.

Maenads: the female devotees of DIONYSUS, and thus
also called BACCHAE, and *Bacchantes*. Inspired by
him to ecstatic frenzy, they accompany him in his
wanderings and as his priestesses carry out his
orgiastic rites. In their wild frenzy they tear animals apart and devour the raw flesh. They are rep-

resented crowned with vine leaves, clothed with fawnskins and carrying the thyrsus, and dancing with the wild abandonment of complete union with primeval nature.

Magna Mater: "the great mother" (of the gods) in Latin, a frequent appellation of RHEA/CYBELE.

Mahadeva: *lit.* "the Great God," an epithet of SHIVA; likewise, PARVATI is *Mahadevi*, 'the Great Goddess."

Maia: one of the PLEIADES, daughters of ATLAS and PLEIONE. She was the eldest and most beautiful, and by ZEUS became the mother of HERMES.

Maitreya: the BUDDHA who is to come in the future. Since he has not yet become a Buddha, he is represented in the costume of a young Indian prince.

Mammon: *lit.* "money," abstract personification of material riches in the Judeo-Christian tradition.

Mana: a term used among the islanders of the South Pacific to denote the supernaturally powerful charge of dynamic energy inherent in the deities and the sacred objects associated with them and their ritual, and which only priests, witch doctors, etc., know how to control. This concept is found in all religions, and has been adopted as a convenient term by anthropologists and students of religions and myth.

Manannan: ancient Celtic sea-god, described as riding over the sea in a chariot.

Manawyddan: Welsh name for MANANNAN.

Manes: in old Latin meaning "good," euphemistic name applied by the Romans to the shades of the

dead, who, as deceased ancestors, were worshipped
as divinities.

Manitu, Manitou, Manito: among the Algonquin
Indians, a general term used to denote various
types of supernatural and/or uncanny beings and
spirits. Among some other American Indian tribes,
the term denotes monstrous or evil creatures. It is
definitely *not* used as an abstraction for a cosmic,
creative power.

Manjusri: in Tibetan Buddhism, the god of wisdom
and learning and bestower of civilization. He is
represented with several arms, seated on a lion and
holding a book, a sword and a thunderbolt. One
of his oldest appellations is "pleasant voice."

Manto: "divination, magic," ancient Greek legendary prophetess, daughter of the seer TIRESIAS and
mother, by the Cretan seer Rhacius or by APOLLO,
of MOPSUS.

Manu: in Hindu myth, the name of the fourteen
legendary ancestors of mankind, and rulers of the
earth. The early Code of Law, probably compiled
during the fourth century B.C., was ascribed to him.
In some sources, *Manu Vaivasvata* is the mortal
who was saved from the Deluge by VISHNU in his
first incarnation as the fish MATSYA.

Marduk: chief god of ancient Babylon, son of EA
(ENKI), who slew TIAMAT, the primeval dragoness
of watery chaos, and became king of the gods. He
then set the universe in order, assigned the gods to
their places and created mankind. He is the *Merodach* of the Old Testament, and his name is also
reflected in that of *Mordecai*.

Mars: Roman god of war, corresponding to the Greek
ARES.

Marsyas: a Phrygian SATYR who found the flute which ATHENA had thrown away because playing upon it distorted her features. He became so proficient upon it that he challenged APOLLO to a musical contest. The MUSES, as judges, decided in favor of Apollo, who punished Marsyas by flaying him alive.

Matsya: in Hindu myth, the first incarnation of the god VISHNU, during which he saved the mortal MANU *Vaivasvata* from the Deluge. The latter found a small fish, which asked his protection. The fish grew rapidly, and Manu recognized it as Vishnu incarnate. At the fish's command, Manu embarked in a ship together with the RISHIS and the seeds of all existing things, and the ship, bound to the fish's great horn, was preserved during the Flood and then rested on a peak of the Himalayas. Matsya later destroyed an underwater demon who had stolen the VEDAS.

Matuta: ancient Roman goddess of the dawn, associated with AURORA and identified with the Greek LEUCOTHEA.

Maui: in Polynesian myth, a sun-god and culture-hero who seized and controlled the forces of nature, and many myths are told of his various adventures. His consort is SINA, the moon-goddess.

Maya: in Hindu belief, the concept or personified goddess of the illusion and unreality of the material world.

Maya: the name of the mother of BUDDHA.

Mazda: see AHURA-MAZDA

Medea: daughter of AEËTES, king of Colchis, famed for her skill in the magic arts, by which she aided

JASON in obtaining the GOLDEN FLEECE. She fled back with him to Thessaly, and after he forsook her for another woman she murdered the two children she had by him.

Medusa: in Greek myth, the only mortal of the three GORGONS, with aspect so terrible that whoever looked upon her was turned to stone. According to one version, she was originally a beautiful maiden, who desecrated ATHENA's temple by lying there with POSEIDON. In revenge, Athena turned her hair into snakes. Her head was cut off by PERSEUS, who presented it to Athena, and the goddess placed it in the center of her AEGIS, which she wore over her breastplate.

Megaera: one of the three FURIES.

Mehturt, or **Mehurt:** ancient Egyptian sky-goddess represented as a colossal cow, along whose belly RA proceeded by day in his solar bark.

Melicertes: son of ATHAMAS and INO. When his mother threw herself into the sea with him, she became the marine deity LEUCOTHEA, and he became the marine deity PALAEMON.

Melpomene: Greek Muse of tragedy, usually represented with tragic mask and wearing the cothurnus. See MUSES.

Memnon: in Greek myth, son of TITHONUS and EOS, and king of the Ethiopians. He was one of the allies of PRIAM of Troy, and was slain in battle by ACHILLES. The so-called *Colossi of Memnon* near Thebes in Egypt (actually huge statues of the fourteenth-century B.C. Egyptian king Amenhotep III) were believed by the Greeks to emit a musical sound when struck by the first rays of the sun: Eos, the dawn-goddess, kissing her son.

Menelaos: son of ATREUS and younger brother of AGAMEMNON. He was king of Sparta, and husband of HELEN, by whom he became the father of HERMIONE. When PARIS, prince of Troy, abducted Helen, Menelaos called upon the aid of his brother Agamemnon, who organized the expedition against Troy.

Mentu (Menthu, Montu, Mont): ancient Egyptian god, patron of war and represented with a falcon's head.

Mercury: Roman name for the Greek god HERMES.

Merodach: Hebrew rendering of MARDUK, in the Old Testament.

Merope: one of the PLEIADES who married a mortal, and for this reason became the faintest star in the constellation.

Mertseger: *lit.* "she who loves silence," in Egyptian myth the patron-goddess of the Theban necropolis, represented as a uraeus-serpent with the head of a woman.

Mesti (Mesta): in ancient Egypt, one of the four "Sons of Horus," represented as human-headed, who guarded the CANOPIC JAR containing the embalmed liver of the deceased.

Metis: personification of "counsel, wisdom," daughter of OCEANUS and TETHYS, and wisest of the deities. She was the first consort of ZEUS, but he swallowed her when he was advised by OURANOS and GAIA that she would bear a child greater than he in wisdom and strength. Zeus had impregnated her, and so he later gave birth to ATHENA, who sprang from his head, fully grown and fully armed.

Midas: legendary king of Phrygia in Asia Minor, who earned the gratitude of DIONYSUS by returning to him the drunken SILENUS who had wandered into his rose gardens. Dionysus promised to grant Midas any wish, and his wish was that everything he touched would turn to gold. When even his food turned to gold, Midas begged the god to take back his gift. Dionysus removed the "golden touch" by having him bathe in the river Pactolus, which ever since has gold in its sands. When Midas decided in favor of PAN as against APOLLO in a musical contest between the two gods, Apollo changed Midas's ears into those of an ass. Midas tried to hide them under his Phrygian cap, but they were discovered by his barber, who, bursting with the secret, dug a hole in the ground and whispered into it, "Midas has ass's ears." He then filled up the hole, but reeds grew on the spot and gave away the secret by their whispers.

Midgard: in Norse myth, the defensive fortress which the gods built about the middle portion of the earth allotted to men in order to protect mankind from the giants.

Midgard Serpent: in Norse myth the serpent JORMUNGAND who encompasses the entire mid-portion of the earth (MIDGARD) and bites its own tail. See OUROBOROS.

Milcom, Milkom: the name is related to the Semitic word for "king" (see also MOLOCH, MOLEKH) ; the god of the Ammonites of the Old Testament, similar in nature to BAAL.

Mimir: in Norse myth, one of the giants and the epitome of wisdom, which he obtained by drinking daily of the "Well of the Highest Wisdom," which was situated near one of the roots of YGGDRASIL.

Min (or Imsu): ancient Egyptian god of fertility and generation, usually represented as ithyphallic, with the tall, double-plumed headdress of AMEN and with his right arm raised and wielding a flagellum. Because of his strong aspects of fertility he was equated with Amen, and as such, the ram was sacred to them both. He was also closely associated with HORUS.

Minerva: Roman goddess corresponding to ATHENA.

Minos: son of ZEUS and EUROPA, and brother of RHAD-AMANTHUS. He was king of Crete, and because of his just laws became one of the judges of the underworld. He was the husband of PASIPHAË, daughter of HELIOS. To avenge the murder of his son Androgeos at Athens, Minos compelled the Athenians to send an annual tribute of seven youths and seven maidens to Knossos to be forced into the LABYRINTH and there to be devoured by the MINOTAUR, the son of Pasiphaë and the bull. He followed DAEDALUS to Sicily after the latter's escape, and was there slain.

Minotaur: a legendary monster, half man and half bull, who was the offspring of PASIPHAË by the bull presented to her husband MINOS by POSEIDON. On his birth, Minos confined the Minotaur in the LABYRINTH, where he was later slain by THESEUS.

Mithra (Mithras): ancient Persian deity, in all likelihood derived from the ancient Indian MITRA mentioned in the VEDAS. In Persia, Mithra was the son of AHURA-MAZDA, identified with the sun, fire, light, etc., with their extensions of goodness, virtue and wisdom, and constantly associated with the sun. He was born from a rock, and his chief task was the slaying of the divine bull, which took place in a cave, after which he ascended to heaven. The cult of Mithra, with its mysteries and initiatory rites, was brought back by the soldiers of Alexander the Great, and later became very popular among the Romans, particularly with the soldiers of the army, who carried the worship with them all over northern Europe and into Britain. Mithraism was an important factor in the later struggle of Paganism with Christianity.

Mitra: in Hindu myth, one of the ADITYAS and a relatively minor deity in the VEDA. As MITHRA, he became the young, active deity in ancient Persia, and associated with AHURA-MAZDA.

Mnemosyne: personified goddess of memory, daughter of OURANOS and GAIA, and by ZEUS mother of the MUSES.

Mnevis: ancient Egyptian sacred bull, regarded as the incarnation of RA and kept at Heliopolis. He is represented with the solar-disc encircled by the uraeus-serpent between his horns.

Moirae (Moerae): original Greek name for the three FATES, or PARCAE.

Moloch, Molekh: *lit.* "king"; one of the deities of the Canaanites mentioned in the Old Testament, a fertility-deity similar to BAAL, and to whom children (usually the firstborn) were sacrificed by fire.

Moly: the mythical herb which HERMES gave to ODYSSEUS to make him immune to the sorceries of CIRCE.

Momus: Greek deity of mockery and faultfinding, called by Hesiod the son of Night (NOX). He found fault with the man made by HEPHAESTUS for not having little doors in his breast through which his secret thoughts might be seen, and with APHRODITE for talking too much and because her sandals creaked.

Mopsus: legendary Greek prophet, son of MANTO and APOLLO (or the Cretan seer Rhacius), and founder of an oracle in Cilicia, after contending with and prevailing over CALCHAS (KALCHAS) in the arts of divination.

Morpheus: *lit.* "he who forms, or molds," so called because he is god of sleep and dreams, fashioning the forms of the sleeper's dreams.

Morrigan: ancient Celtic goddess of fertility, war and magic, whose name means "queen of the demons," and like many fertility goddesses, associated with rivers. She was united in sacred marriage with the DAGDA.

Mors: personified god of death among the Romans, a translation of THANATOS, which see.

Mot: *lit.* "Death"; personified deity of death in ancient Syria-Palestine, and the great adversary of BAAL. Mot slays Baal, but is in turn killed and cut to pieces by the fertility-goddess ANATH, who then revives her lover, Baal.

Mulciber: *lit.* "the softener" in Latin, a surname of VULCAN (HEPHAESTUS) and alluding to the softening of metals in the smith-god's fiery forge.

Mummu: ancient Sumero-Babylonian craftsman-god, and personification of technical skill, attendant upon EA (ENKI). Mummu had been the vizier of TIAMAT and APSU, and Enki, after slaying the latter, bound Mummu into his service.

Muses: Greek goddesses of literature, music, the dance and intellectual pursuits in general, who inspire their devotees to creative activity, and are often led by APOLLO. The nine Muses are the daughters of ZEUS and MNEMOSYNE, and were born at Pieria, at the foot of Mt. Olympus. They are: CALLIOPE, Muse of epic poetry; CLIO, Muse of history; EUTERPE, Muse of lyric poetry and music; TERPSICHORE, Muse of choral dance and song; ERATO, Muse of erotic poetry and the mime; MELPOMENE, Muse of tragedy; THALIA, Muse of comedy; POLYHYMNIA, Muse of the sacred hymn; URANIA, Muse of astronomy. In the literature, they are associated with Pieria, their birthplace, with Mt. Helicon and with Mt. Parnassus.

Muspellsheim: in Norse myth, the flaming, torrid region, the "Home of Desolation" opposed to NIFLHEIM, and from whose animating beams sprang the first living beings. The celestial bodies were made from its sparks which flew out into space.

Mut: *lit.* "mother" in ancient Egyptian, the consort of the god AMEN. She was originally a vulture-goddess, and is depicted either as a vulture, or in the form of a woman wearing a vulture headdress and the double crown of Egypt.

Mutinus: a Roman form of the Greek PRIAPUS.

Mylitta: Babylonian goddess mentioned by Herodotus, who relates that every Babylonian woman had, at least once in her life, to consort with a stranger within the precincts of the temple of Mylitta, whom he equates with APHRODITE. She was paid for this, and the money thus earned was dedicated to the goddess. Mylitta is to be identified with ISHTAR / ASTARTE.

Myrmidons: the inhabitants of Thessaly, who accompanied their chief ACHILLES to Troy. Their ancestors were supposed to have been ants which were changed to men.

N

Nabu (or Nebo): ancient Sumero-Babylonian god of writing and knowledge and the scribe of the gods, and regarded as the son of MARDUK.

Nagas: in Hindu myth, a primeval race of divine serpent-people, ruled over by SESHA.

Naiads: Greek NYMPHS who dwell in fresh waters, such as rivers, brooks and springs. Many Naiads of springs inspire those who drink of them. One of these, however, may have an interesting but somewhat deleterious effect (SALMACIS).

Nakshatras: in Hindu myth, the stars, the divine attendants upon INDRA.

Namtar: ancient Sumero-Babylonian underworld god, regarded as the messenger of ERESHKIGAL and the herald of death, bringing plagues and diseases.

Nannar: early Sumerian name for the moon-god better known by his Babylonian name of SIN, which see.

Narayana: in Hindu myth, the original Supreme Being who lies on the body of SHESANAGA, the huge serpent on the Ocean of Milk. In some sources he is identified with the original man, and in others with VISHNU, which see.

Narcissus: a beautiful youth, beloved by ECHO. He did not return her love, and she pined away until only her voice remained. He fell in love with his own image reflected in a fountain pool and died of frustration at not being able to satisfy his desire. This is given either as the cause of his refusal of the love of Echo, or as the punishment for his refusal.

Nectar: the drink of which the Greek gods partake, together with AMBROSIA.

Nefertem (Nefertum): ancient Egyptian god identified with the lotus, son of PTAH and SEKHMET, and represented as wearing upon his head a lotus flower surmounted by two tall plumes.

Neit (Neith): ancient Egyptian goddess of Sais in the Delta, wearing the crown of Lower Egypt and holding a bow and arrows or with crossed arrows upon her head.

Nekhbet: the patron-goddess of Upper Egypt (below the Delta of the Nile), symbolized by the vulture and depicted wearing the crown of Upper Egypt.

Nemesis: ancient Greek personification of divine anger toward human transgression of the natural, right order of things and of the arrogance causing it, pursuing the insolent and the wicked with inflexible vengeance. The epithet ADRASTEIA (ADRASTEA), "she whom none can escape," properly one of those of the Phrygian RHEA CYBELE, was later applied to her.

Nephele: wife of ATHAMAS, who married her at the command of HERA, and by him the mother of PHRIXUS and HELLE. She saved her children from the intrigues of INO by placing them on the back of the ram with the GOLDEN FLEECE, who flew away with them over the sea.

Nephthys: ancient Egyptian goddess, daughter of GEB and NUT and sister of OSIRIS, ISIS and SET. She is sometimes mentioned as consort of Set, but is usually depicted and mentioned in association with Isis, lamenting Osiris with her after his death, and with her in attendance upon him in the Land of Eternity.

Neptune: Roman god of the sea, equated with POSEIDON.

Nereids: Greek nymphs who dwell in the Mediterranean Sea. They are the fifty daughters of NEREUS and DORIS, daughter of OCEANUS.

Nereus: son OCEANUS and GAIA, and father of the NEREIDS by DORIS. He is described as the righteous and all-wise "old man of the sea." Like other marine deities, he was believed to have the power of prophecy and to assume any form he chooses.

Nergal: ancient Sumero-Babylonian deity, sometimes regarded as representing the sinister aspects of the sun-god SHAMASH, sending war, pestilence and devastation, and sometimes as the consort of ERESHKIGAL, ruler of the nether world.

Nerthus (Hertha): ancient Teutonic earth and fertility deity, possibly hermaphroditic in nature, sometimes connected with NJORD.

Nessus: a CENTAUR, who when HERACLES with his wife DEIANIRA were crossing the river Evenus, bore Deianira across on his back and attempted to violate her. Heracles then shot Nessus with a poisoned arrow. The dying Centaur told Deianira to take his blood and use it as a means to preserving her husband's love. She later impregnated a tunic of Heracles with the poisoned blood, which burned his flesh and caused him such agony that he had himself burned alive on a pyre.

Niblungs (Niebelungs): see NIFLUNGS

Nidhogg: in Norse myth, the monstrous serpent which, together with other serpents, gnaws continually at the deepest roots of YGGDRASIL, threatening to destroy it.

Niflheim: in Norse myth, the far northern region of icy fogs and mist.

Niflungs, Niblungs, Niebelungs: in Norse myth, the royal family whose queen, GRIMHILD, enchants SIGURD so that he marries her daughter GUDRUN. In the later Teutonic version of the story, the Niflungs (Niblungs) are represented as the dwellers in NIFLHEIM.

Nike: personified Greek goddess of Victory, daughter of PALLAS and STYX and sister of ZELUS, CRATOS and BIA.

Nikkal: ancient Syro-Palestinian moon-goddess, the Mesopotamian NINGAL.

Nilus: Graeco-Roman personified god of the river Nile. In Egyptian he was called HAPI.

Ningal: *lit.* "the great lady," ancient Sumero-Akkadian moon-goddess and consort of SIN. In Ur, she and Sin were regarded as the parents of SHAMASH and ISHTAR.

Ningirsu: ancient Sumero-Babylonian god of rain and fertility, son of ENLIL and patron deity of the ancient Sumerian city of Lagash. His consort is BABA.

Ninhursag: *lit.* "lady of the great mountain," early Sumero-Babylonian mother goddess, associated with the triad of ANU, ENLIL and EA (ENKI), as goddess of childbirth, and connected with the creation of mankind. She is also referred to as NINMAH, NINTU and ARURU.

Ninib: former, erroneous reading of the name of the Mesopotamian deity NINURTA.

Ninlil: ancient Sumero-Babylonian mother and fertility goddess, consort of ENLIL. See NINHURSAG.

Ninmah: see NINHURSAG

Nintu: see NINHURSAG

Ninurta: ancient Sumero Babylonian god of rain and fertility, son of ENLIL, and frequently confused with NINGIRSU.

Niobe: daughter of TANTALUS, sister of PELOPS and wife of AMPHION, king of Thebes. She had six (or seven) sons and an equal number of daughters, and boasted of her superiority to LETO, who had only two: APOLLO and ARTEMIS. In punishment for this arrogance, all her children were slain by the arrows of the children of Leto, the sons being slain by Apollo and the daughters by Artemis.

Nirvana: in Buddhism, the final state of release of the soul from the causality of eternal rebirths (KARMA), a beatific state in which desires will have lost their effect.

Nixes: in Norse myth, the water-sprites who live in

rivers and lakes. They were considered as malignant in some quarters, but as harmless and friendly in others.

Njord: in Norse myth, a god of the winds, sea and fire, governing good fortune at sea and in the hunt.

Norns: in Norse myth, the goddesses of destiny, controlling not only the fates of both men and gods, but also the unchanging laws of the cosmos. Their names are *Urd, Verdandi* and *Skuld,* and they dwell beside a well under the branches of YGG-DRASIL.

Notus: Greek god of the South Wind, son of the TITAN Astraeus and EOS, and brother of BOREAS, EURUS and ZEPHYRUS. In Latin, AUSTER.

Novensiles: the Roman appellation of the nine great gods of the Etruscans.

Nox (or Nyx): personification of Night, born of the primeval CHAOS in the ancient Greek cosmology.

Numa Pompilius: successor of ROMULUS and second king of early Rome. He was celebrated for his piety and his introduction of wise legislation and the forms of worship, and was believed to have been guided in these matters by the nymph EGERIA.

Nun (Nu): in ancient Egyptian theology, the mass of primeval waters which existed before creation, and from which RA-ATUM-KHEPRI emerged self-created.

Nusku: in Sumero-Akkadian myth the god of fire, and sometimes regarded as the son of SIN and NIN-GAL. He consumed the sacrifices on the altars and made them pleasing to the gods. In this capacity he was often regarded as the intermediary between the gods, particularly ANU and ENLIL, and men.

Nut: ancient Egyptian personified goddess of the sky, with her consort GEB (Earth) the children of SHU and TEFNUT. Nut is usually represented as nude, her body covered with stars and stretching over the earth, sometimes held up by Shu (Air). By Geb, she is the mother of OSIRIS, ISIS, SET and NEPHTHYS.

Nymphs: Greek goddesses who dwell in the various places of wild nature, such as mountains, grottoes, forests, groves and trees, rivers and springs and the ocean. They are represented as young and pretty girls who frolic about with the SATYRS, PAN and the SILENI in the train of DIONYSUS, and nymphs also range with ARTEMIS (DIANA) in her hunt. Often benevolent to mankind in the places where they dwell, they will, however, take away with them those mortals to whom they take a fancy, and visit with dire punishment those unresponsive to their love. Nymphs of groves and forests are HAMADRY-ADS; nymphs of mountains and grottoes are OREADS; nymphs of fresh waters, such as springs, rivers, etc., are NAIADS; nymphs of the sea are NEREIDS; and those of the ocean are OCEANIDS.

Nyx: see NOX

O

Oannes: Greek rendering of the Sumero-Babylonian EA (ENKI), because of his connection with the waters sometimes depicted as half man, half fish.

Oberon: in some medieval folklore, the king of the fairies, TITANIA being his queen.

Oceanids: nymphs of the great ocean, daughters of OCEANUS.

Oceanus: Greek deity of the great ocean encircling the earth. He was one of the TITANS, the son of OURANOS (Sky) and GAIA (Earth), and husband of TETHYS, by whom he was the father of the OCEANIDS, or ocean-nymphs, and the various rivers and river-gods.

Ocypete: one of the three HARPIES.

Odin (Woden, Wotan): in Norse myth the supreme deity, son of BORR and *Bestla*, daughter of one of the primeval giants, who bore Odin, VILI and VE. Odin and his brothers created the cosmos and all animate things, including ASK and EMBLA, the first human pair, whom they created from two trees. As chief of the AESIR, Odin presided over the assemblage of the gods and over their feasts, consuming nothing but wine. He was also the wisest of the gods, and derived his wisdom from two ravens (their names being *Hugin,* "thought," and *Munin,* "memory") who perched on his shoulders and flew through all the reaches of the universe and told him what they had seen. He had given one of his eyes in pawn to MIMIR so that he might imbibe wisdom from his well, and hence was also referred to as "one-eyed." He was also a god of battles, and captured enemies were sometimes sacrificed to him. He had many concubines, but his chief wife was FRIGG.

Odysseus: son of Laertes and king of the island of Ithaca, and one of the leaders of the Achaeans in the Trojan War. The *Odyssey* of Homer describes his various adventures on his journey homeward after the fall of Troy, his wanderings being caused by the wrath of POSEIDON, whose son POLYPHEMUS Odysseus and his men had blinded. After adventures at the island of AEOLUS, with the nymph CALYPSO, with the sorceress CIRCE, etc., he arrived home after twenty years in the guise of an old beggar and slew the suitors of his wife PENELOPE, who had remained faithful to him.

Oedipus: son of LAIUS, king of Thebes, and his queen JOCASTA. Laius, learning from an oracle that he was destined to be killed by his own son, ordered the infant Oedipus to be exposed on Mt. Cithaeron. He was found by a herdsman, who took him to his master, King Polybus of Corinth, who reared him as his own. When he was grown he visited Delphi, where the oracle told him that he would kill his father and marry his mother. Thinking that Polybus was his father, Oedipus did not return to Corinth, but went to Thebes. He met his unknown father Laius on the road and killed him during a scuffle. He then solved the riddle of the SPHINX which was plaguing Thebes, and was awarded the kingship of Thebes and the widowed Jocasta to wife. When he discovered his true parentage and the fact that he had been cohabiting with his mother, he put out his own eyes, and Jocasta hanged herself.

Ogma: in Celtic myth, one of the champion leaders of the TUATHA DE DANANN, sometimes regarded as the son of DAGDA, and the reputed inventor of the ancient Celtic alphabet called *Ogham*.

Olympus: the mountain range between Macedonia and Thessaly in northern Greece, where ZEUS and his generation of gods had their palaces.

Omphalos: *lit.* "navel," the reputed center of the earth, and the sacred oval or hemispherical stone marking the spot, at the temple of APOLLO at Delphi. According to the myth, ZEUS determined the spot by sending forth two eagles simultaneously to fly from the eastern and western ends of the earth, and they met at Delphi.

Oneiros: ancient Greek personified deity of dreams, which are regarded by Homer as dwelling on the shores of Ocean in the extreme west. Deceptive dreams issue from a gate of ivory and true dreams issue from a gate of horn.

Oni: the demonic powers of evil, assuming various forms, in Japanese myth.

Onouris (Onuris): Greek rendering of the ancient Egyptian *In-hert,* a sky-god often identified with SHU, represented as holding a spear aloft and with four tall plumes on his head.

Ophion: *lit.* "the serpent," one of the TITANS. In one tradition, Ophion and his consort Eurynome, "the wide-ruling," reigned over Olympus until they were dethroned by the younger generation of gods.

Opochitl: in Aztec myth, the god of fishing and bird snaring.

Ops: "plenty," personification of the ancient Roman goddesses of the earth and fertility, and with her other personifications, TELLUS, TERRA, FAUNA, usually called the BONA DEA.

Oracles: the places sacred to certain divinities who would inspire their priests or priestesses into a state of ecstasy in which they would utter prophecies. The most famous oracles were those of APOLLO at Delphi, of ZEUS at Dodona, and of AESCULAPIUS at Epidaurus.

Orcus: one of the Roman names for HADES, both for the god and for his domains.

Oreads: the Greek NYMPHS of mountains and grottoes.

Orenda: the invisible animistic power believed by the Iroquois Indians to reside in all things. Like MANA, the term has been adopted by anthropologists for general technical use.

Orestes: son of AGAMEMNON and CLYTEMNESTRA and brother of ELECTRA and IPHIGENIA. He was a child when Agamemnon was murdered by his wife and her paramour AEGISTHUS, and Electra saved him by secretly sending him to be brought up in Phocis. He later returned, and at the instigation of Electra slew Aegisthus and his mother, for which he was driven mad and pursued by the FURIES. He was rescued from them by the counsel of ATHENA. According to another tradition, he had to fetch the statue of ARTEMIS from Taurus, whither he went accompanied by his faithful friend Pylades. When they arrived there, they were seized as strangers to be sacrificed to the goddess, but were recognized by Iphigenia, who was the priestess, and all three escaped with the statue. They returned home to Mycenae and Orestes took possession of his kingdom and married HERMIONE, daughter of MENELAOS.

Orion: a giant hunter, variously stated to be a companion and/or lover of ARTEMIS, or slain by her arrows when attempting to rape her. After his death, he became a constellation in the sky.

Ormazd, Ormuzd: see AHURA-MAZDA

Orpheus: son of Oeagrus king of Thrace (or of APOLLO) and the MUSE CALLIOPE. Apollo presented him with the lyre, with which he made such enchanting music that he charmed the wild beasts and made the trees and rocks move. His newly wedded wife EURYDICE was killed by a serpent bite, and Orpheus descended into the realms of HADES to fetch her back. There he so charmed the rulers of the underworld by his music that he was allowed to lead Eurydice back to earth on condition that he would not look back upon her until they had reached the upper world. But at the last moment his desire overcame him, he looked back, and Eurydice was lost to him forever. In his grief for her he lost all interest in women, and charmed the Thracian men with his music. In revenge the women of Thrace tore him to pieces during their Bacchic revels. His head was carried by the river Hebrus to the sea, by which it was brought, still singing, to the island of Lesbos, which became the first renowned seat of lyric poetry. The Mysteries of Orpheus were assimilated to those of DIONYSUS, the Orphic-Dionysiac myth centering about Dionysus as ZAGREUS, and later adding many Eastern mystic elements.

Osiris: ancient Egyptian god of fertility and lord of the afterworld. He was the eldest child of GEB (Earth) and NUT (Sky) and as such was given lordship over the earth and was the first king of Egypt, ruling beneficently with his sister and consort ISIS, and teaching mankind the arts of agriculture. His evil brother SET, jealous of his prerogatives, ambushed and slew him, and then either cast his body into the Nile or cut it into pieces, scattering the parts throughout the provinces of Egypt. Isis, with her sister NEPHTHYS, bewailed the dead Osiris, and then Isis searched for and finally found Osiris's body and by means of her magic power resuscitated or reconstituted it, and was able to infuse enough life into Osiris so that he could impregnate her. Then he departed to the other world, becoming Lord of Eternity and ruler over the departed, who must come before Osiris for judgment when they enter his domains. Isis gave birth to their child HORUS, who when he attained manhood engaged Set in a mighty and bloody struggle for the kingdom. He proved victorious over Set, and the council of the gods adjudged Osiris "true of voice," or the justified legitimate ruler of Egypt, and Horus as his heir. In Old Kingdom times (about 2700–2200 B.C.) the deceased king became Osiris after his death, and his heir on the throne the living Horus. During the Middle Kingdom (2100–1900 B.C.) the nobles, and during the New Kingdom and later (after 1550 B.C.) even commoners who could afford the necessary funerary rituals could also become Osiris, but at all times only the king was the living Horus.

Osiris was usually depicted as mummiform, wearing a very ornate headdress and holding the crook-scepter and the flail, symbols of the royal power. His flesh is colored green or black, the color of the earth and hence of fertility.

Ostara: see EASTRE

Otus: one of the two giant ALOIDAE, who attempted to scale the heavens and dethrone ZEUS.

Ouranos, Uranus: personification of the sky, and son and mate of GAIA, the earth. Their children were the HEKATONCHEIRES, the CYCLOPES, the FURIES and the TITANS. He was jealous of the future power of his children and confined them in TARTARUS. At the instigation of Gaia, the Titan KRONOS castrated his father Ouranos and dethroned him.

Ouroboros, Uroboros: *lit.* "the tail-devourer," a representation of a serpent with its tail in its mouth, and used to symbolize concepts of completion, perfection and totality, the endless round of existence, etc.

P

Palaemon: a marine deity connected with POSEIDON, and identified by the Romans with PORTUNUS, god of harbors. He was originally MELICERTES, son of INO, and became a marine deity together with his mother when she cast herself with him into the sea.

Pales: Roman deity, variously male or female, patron of shepherds and presiding over the fertility of domestic animals. The name is believed by some to be related to the Greek and Latin word *phallus*.

Palladium: a small, ancient wooden image of PALLAS ATHENA preserved at Troy, and believed to have fallen from heaven. The Trojans believed that as long as the image was preserved within the city, Troy would be safe. It was secretly stolen by ODYSSEUS, and Troy fell to the Achaeans shortly thereafter.

Pallas: one of the Greek TITANS, and by STYX the father of ZELUS, BIA and NIKE. Also an appellation of the goddess ATHENA, who according to some accounts was the daughter of Pallas. In this version, she killed him when he attempted to violate her, and his skin became the AEGIS.

Pan: Greek nature and fertility deity, originally native to Arcadia. As such, he is god of goatherds and flocks, and is usually represented as a very sensual creature, a shaggy human to the loins, with pointed ears, goat's horns and legs. He wanders among the mountains and valleys, pursuing the NYMPHS or leading them in their dances. He is quite musical, and is the inventor of the *Syrinx*, or "Pipes of Pan." He is considered to be a son of HERMES.

Panacaea: "heal-all," or "universal cure," a daughter of the AESCULAPIUS, patron deity of the healing arts.

Pandora: the first woman on earth, whom ZEUS caused HEPHAESTUS to form from the earth to bring misery upon humanity in revenge for the theft of the heavenly fire by PROMETHEUS. The deities endowed her with their various gifts, and hence she was called Pandora, "all-gifted." She was given a box (or jar) which she was told not to open, containing all the evils which beset humanity, and presented to EPIMETHEUS, brother of Prometheus, as his wife. Impelled by her natural curiosity, Pandora opened her box, and all the evils it contained escaped and spread over the earth. However, the box contained one good, Hope, which remained behind.

Pandrosos: "the all-dewy one," a daughter of CECROPS.

Pan-Ku: in Chinese myth, a giant who came into being from the YANG and the YIN. He shaped the world out of CHAOS, or the universe was formed from his body. He is depicted by the Taoists as a shaggy primitive being bearing a huge hammer with which he breaks up the primeval. rocks.

Parcae: Roman name for the three FATES.

Paris: son of PRIAM and HECUBA, king and queen of Troy. On the occasion of the marriage of PELEUS and THETIS, all the deities were invited, except ERIS, the goddess of strife. Enraged, she threw among the guests a golden apple, upon which was engraved

"To the fairest." The contention as to which goddess deserved the golden apple narrowed down to HERA, ATHENA and APHRODITE. Paris, as a well-known and handsome playboy, was called in to judge among them. Each of the these goddesses offered him bribes, Hera offering power, Athena fame in war, and Aphrodite the most beautiful woman in the world. Paris naturally decided in favor of Aphrodite, and she arranged his visit to MENELAOS and his abduction of HELEN, which brought about the Trojan War. At the fall of Troy, Paris was wounded and asked his wife Oenone to heal him. She refused, and he died. Oenone killed herself in remorse.

Parnassus: a mountain in Greece sacred to APOLLO and the MUSES, and upon which rested the ark built by DEUCALION.

Parthenos: "virgin," an epithet of the goddess ATHENA. The *Parthenon* is her temple on the Acropolis in Athens.

Parvati: in Hindu myth, one of the appellations of the consort of SHIVA, in her aspect as mountain-goddess. See DEVI.

Pasiphaë: daughter of HELIOS and sister of CIRCE. She became the wife of MINOS, king of Crete, and by him the mother of Androgeos, ARIADNE and PHAEDRA. She fell in love with a beautiful white bull presented to Minos by POSEIDON, and in order to attract the bull, crept inside an ingeniously life-like hollow cow of wood which she had ordered DAEDALUS, the master craftsman, to fashion. As result of her union with the bull, she gave birth to the MINOTAUR.

Patroclus: the intimate friend of ACHILLES, with

whom he was brought up at the court of PELEUS. He accompanied Achilles to Troy, and was killed by HECTOR. The desire to avenge his friend's death caused Achilles to return to the fighting whence he had withdrawn because of his feud with AGAMEMNON.

Pax: "peace," personified Roman goddess corresponding to the Greek EIRENE.

Pegasus: the fabulous winged horse which sprang from the blood of MEDUSA after PERSEUS had severed her head. Medusa had been made pregnant by POSEIDON, who is thus considered the father of Pegasus. With the aid of a golden bridle, the gift of ATHENA, Pegasus was caught by BELLEROPHON, who flew upon him to kill the CHIMAERA.

Pele: in Polynesian myth, the Hawaiian fire-goddess who bursts the volcanoes and submerges islands under the seas.

Peleus: king of the Myrmidons at Phthia in Thessaly, and husband of THETIS, one of the NEREIDS. ZEUS wished to be Thetis's lover, but on hearing the prophecy of THEMIS that the son of Thetis would be more illustrious than his father, Zeus wedded her to Peleus, by whom she later became the mother of ACHILLES. At the wedding of Peleus and Thetis occurred the incident which resulted in the Trojan War. See PARIS.

Pelias: son of POSEIDON and king of Iolcus. He seized the throne from its rightful heir, his half brother AESON. When Aeson's son JASON later came to claim the throne, Pelias, in order to rid himself of him, sent him to fetch the GOLDEN FLEECE from Colchis. After Jason's return, Pelias was cut to pieces and boiled by his own daughters, who had been told by MEDEA that thus they might restore his youth.

Pelops: son of TANTALUS, king of Phrygia. Tantalus was a favorite of the gods, and once invited them all to a banquet. Thinking to test their omniscience, Tantalus served them the flesh of his son Pelops, whom he had cut to pieces and boiled. The gods detected the ruse and all abstained except DEMETER who, abstracted by the loss of her daughter PERSEPHONE, ate one of his shoulders. At the behest of ZEUS, HERMES put the limbs of Pelops into into a cauldron, from which Pelops came forth alive once more, and perfect except for the shoulder consumed by Demeter, who thereupon supplied him with a shoulder of ivory. Pelops later became king in Elis, in the Peloponnesus, and father of, among others, ATREUS and THYESTES.

Pemphredo: "alarm," one of the GRAIAE.

Penates: *lit.* "the inner ones," the Roman household gods who presided over the welfare of the family, and kept in the innermost, central part of the house. Among them were included the LARES, or deified spirits of the family ancestors.

Penelope: wife of ODYSSEUS, and celebrated for her loyalty to him during his long absence. She was importuned by many suitors, who wished to seize the kingdom of Ithaca, and she continually put them off by declaring that she must first finish weaving a shroud for Laertes, the aged father of Odysseus. She would unravel by night what she had woven by day, and thus kept the suitors off until her secret was betrayed, but Odysseus arrived soon after.

Peneus: god of a river in Thessaly, son of OCEANUS

and TETHYS, and father of DAPHNE, the nymph who was pursued by APOLLO.

Penthesilea: daughter of ARES and queen of the AMAZONS. She fought against the Achaeans as an ally of Troy, but was slain by ACHILLES, who mourned the beauty, youth and valor of the dying warrior-queen.

Pentheus: son of AGAVE, daughter of CADMUS king of Thebes. He succeeded to the kingdom, and violently opposed the introduction of the worship of DIONYSUS. The god then drove his mother into a mad Bacchic frenzy, and in the company of the reveling MAENADS, she tore her own son to pieces.

Peris: in ancient Persian myth, female spirits who are either among the demons of AHRIMAN or beneficent goddesses associated with Heaven.

Perkunas: Lithuanian thunder and lightning god, identified with PEROUN (PERUN).

Peroun, Perun: Slavonic thunder-god with fiery face, who drives across the sky hurling shafts of lightning. He is associated with the oak, and a fire of oak wood burned continually before his image.

Persephone: daughter of ZEUS and DEMETER, and frequently called KORE ("the daughter," "the maiden"). She was beloved by HADES, and abducted by him to be his consort in the underworld. Her mother Demeter searched for her disconsolately, leaving the earth barren, until it was decreed that Persephone should spend part of the year with her. The rites of Demeter and Persephone ("the Mother and the Daughter") were central to the Eleusinian Mysteries in Attica.

Perseus: Greek legendary hero, son of ZEUS and

DANAË. Polydectes, king of the Aegean island of Seriphos, fell in love with Danaë and in order to get rid of Perseus, sent him to fetch the head of the GORGON MEDUSA. He stole the single eye and tooth of the GRAIAE, the sisters of the Gorgons, and refused to return them until they aided him in reaching Medusa. He found the Gorgons asleep and cut off the head of Medusa, looking at her reflection in a mirror to avoid being turned into stone. After further adventures, including the rescue of ANDROMEDA from the sea-dragon, he came back to Polydectes and turned him into stone. He then presented the Gorgon's head to ATHENA, who set it in the middle of her AEGIS.

Phaedra: daughter of MINOS and PASIPHAË of Crete, and younger sister of ARIADNE. THESEUS later married her and took her with him to Athens. She fell in love with HIPPOLYTUS, son of Theseus by ANTIOPE, the Amazonian queen. When Hippolytus refused to accede to her desires she hanged herself, leaving a note accusing him of having seduced her.

Phaëthon: *lit.* "the shining one," an epithet of HELIOS (the Sun) but according to the more commonly known myth the son of Helios by CLYMENE. Phaëthon induced his father Helios to allow him to drive the chariot of the sun across the heavens for one day. The horses, feeling their reins held by a weaker hand, ran wildly out of their course and came close to the earth, almost destroying it by fire. Thereupon ZEUS slew him with his lightning bolt.

Phallus, Phallos: a Greek term used to denote the masculine sexual organs, particularly as a concrete symbol of the principle of generation, rebirth and ongoing life. As such, it was (and is) used in many rituals of the fertility religions, notably those of the rituals of the ancient Near East and the Aegean world. See also LINGA, YONI.

Philyra: an OCEANID, and by KRONOS the mother of CHIRON the CENTAUR.

Phlegethon: a river of fire, one of the rivers in the realms of HADES.

Phobos: *lit.* "fright," sometimes considered as a son of ARES, and accompanying him in battle.

Phoebe: one of the female TITANS, and by her brother Coeus, mother of LETO, who in turn became by ZEUS the mother of APOLLO and ARTEMIS. The latter are also accorded the appellations Phoebus and Phoebe.

Phoebus: *lit.* "the shining one," an epithet of APOLLO because of his connection with the sun or as descendant of the Titaness PHOEBE.

Phoenix: the fabulous *bennu* bird of ancient Egyptian myth, associated with the god RA. According to Classical writers, the Phoenix lived for five hundred years, after which it consumed itself upon a burning pyre of aromatic wood, and from its ashes a young Phoenix arose.

Phorcydes: the offspring of PHORCYS and CETO: the GRAIAE, the GORGONS and ECHIDNA.

Phorcys: son of OCEANUS and GAIA. By his sister CETO he became the father of the PHORCYDES.

Phrixus: son of ATHAMAS, king of Thebes, and NEPHELE, and brother of HELLE. At the instigation of his stepmother INO, Phrixus was to be sacrificed to ZEUS, but he and his sister were saved by their mother and placed on the back of the golden ram given to her by HERMES. The ram flew away with them over the sea, but Helle fell off its back and was drowned. Phrixus arrived safely at Colchis, where he was received by King AEËTES, who sacrificed the ram to Zeus, and had its GOLDEN FLEECE guarded by a dragon. The fleece was later carried off by JASON.

Picus: ancient Roman agricultural divinity, possessed of the powers of prophecy. When he did not requite the passion of CIRCE, she changed him into a woodpecker.

Picumnus and **Pilumnus:** two ancient rustic Latin gods of the fertility of the fields and of the use of grain, and hence patrons of matrimony.

Pillars of Hercules: the rocky heights on both sides of the Straits of Gibraltar. In one tradition, it was HERACLES who broke through the mountain barrier which had locked the Mediterranean, thus creating the outlet to the ocean.

Pleiades: the seven daughters of ATLAS and PLEIONE. They were the virgin companions of ARTEMIS. Pursued, together with their mother, by ORION, they prayed for rescue to the gods. Their prayer was answered, and they were changed into doves and later into stars, forming a constellation in the sky.

Pleione: one of the OCEANIDS, and by ATLAS the mother of the seven PLEIADES.

Pluto, Ploutos: see HADES

Plutus: god of wealth, son of ZEUS and the OCEANID Electra, and brother of BOOTES. He is said to have been blinded by Zeus, that he might dispense his gifts blindly and without regard to merit.

Pluvius: *lit.* "sender of rain," an epithet of the Roman JUPITER.

Polias: *lit.* "of the city (*polis*)," and epithet of ATHENA as protectress of the Acropolis and of the city of Athens.

Pollux: better-known Roman name for the Greek legendary hero-divinity POLYDEUCES, brother of CASTOR and one of the "Heavenly Twins." See DIOSCURI.

Polyhymnia: Greek Muse of the sacred hymn, usually represented in a pensive or meditating attitude. See MUSES.

Polyphemus: one of the CYCLOPES, son of POSEIDON, who dwelt near Mt. Aetna in Sicily. ODYSSEUS and his men fell into his clutches, and the Cyclops imprisoned them in his cave. After he had devoured several of Odysseus's companions, Odysseus succeeded in getting him drunk and putting out his only eye with the sharpened and heated trunk of a tree. The prisoners then escaped by clinging to the bellies of Polyphemus's sheep as they filed out of the cave.

Pomona: ancient Latin goddess presiding over fruit trees. She was beloved of the ancient Roman rustic deities such as SILVANUS, PICUS and VERTUMNUS.

Popol Vuh: a collection of sacred writings of the Indians of pre-Columbian Central America. It means "The Book of Written Leaves," and contains creation myths, the wars of the gods with the giants, the exploits of the legendary heroes, etc.

Porphyrion: one of the GIANTS who fought against the gods.

Portunus: the Roman god of ports and harbors, identified with the Greek PALAEMON.

Poseidon: Greek god of the sea, and creator of waters, the son of KRONOS and RHEA and brother of ZEUS and HADES. As lord of the pounding waves, he splits the earth and rocks with his trident, and his frequent epithet in Homer is "the earth-shaker." His power of making the earth quake also explains his attribute as ruler of horses. Dolphins and bulls are also sacred to him. His mate was the NEREID AMPHITRITE. He was equated by the Romans with their sea-god NEPTUNE.

Prajapatis: in Hindu myth, divine creatures who proceeded from the mind of BRAHMA, a name applied to some of the deities, but particularly identified with the RISHIS.

Priam: king of Troy at the period of the Trojan War, and husband of HECUBA (HEKABE). PARIS and HECTOR are the best known of his fifty sons. After ACHILLES had slain Hector, Priam went to the former's tent to ransom his son's body in order to give it proper burial. Achilles finally surrendered it, after one of the most dramatic and moving scenes in the entire *Iliad*.

Priapus: son of DIONYSUS and APHRODITE, and a strongly phallic fertility-deity. He was regarded as protector of gardens and domestic animals and fruits, and carved images of Priapus, with large, ithyphallic genitals, were placed in the fields and gardens to ensure fruitfulness and protection.

Prithivi: in Hindu myth, one of the divine attendants upon INDRA. The word means "earth," and may possibly denote an earth-goddess.

Procrustes: *lit.* "the stretcher," legendary robber of ancient Attica. He bound his victims to a bed, and if they were shorter than the bed he stretched their limbs until they would fit. If their limbs were longer, he lopped them off. He was slain by THESEUS.

Prometheus: son of the TITAN IAPETOS and the OCEANID CLYMENE. He was brother of ATLAS, Menoetius and EPIMETHEUS. His name is taken to signify "forethought." He taught mankind the useful arts and crafts, and particularly the use of fire, which had been jealously guarded by ZEUS. Prometheus stole fire from Olympus, hiding it in the hollow fennel-reed, and brought it down to man. For this Zeus cast him out from Olympus and had him fastened to a rock on the Caucasus, where by day an eagle (or a vulture) fed on his liver, which grew again during the night. After many thousands of years, the eagle was killed by HERACLES, and Prometheus was set free. According to Aeschylus, Prometheus's mother is THEMIS. She had revealed to him her prophecy concerning the son of THETIS, and it is this secret which Prometheus holds out to Zeus as the price of his freedom. According to some traditions Prometheus had been the creator of man, whom he formed out of earth and water.

Proserpina: Roman name of PERSEPHONE.

Proteus: a prophetic sea divinity, son of either POSEIDON or OCEANUS, who would foretell the future to those who could seize him. When caught, he would assume all possible varying forms so as to avoid prophesying, but when held fast despite it all, he assumed his usual form of an old man and told the truth.

Protogonus: appellation of EROS, in the theology of the Orphic-Dionysiac Mysteries, as "firstborn" of the cosmic egg of NOX (Night).

Psyche: *lit.* "the soul," in Classical legend a king's daughter who was so beautiful as to arouse the jealousy of APHRODITE. The goddess sent her son EROS to excite her to the love of the ugliest of men, but he fell in love with her himself. He carried her off to a fabulous palace where he visited her only by night, warning her not to attempt to learn his appearance. Her curiosity aroused by her jealous sisters, one night Psyche lighted a lamp while the god was sleeping by her side and gazed upon his beauty, but a drop of the hot oil from the lamp fell upon his shoulder, arousing him. He upbraided her furiously and then disappeared. Psyche wandered everywhere in search of him until she came to the temple of Aphrodite, who imposed upon her all sorts of the most difficult tasks. Eros aided her secretly, and after she thus accomplished all her labors, Aphrodite's hatred was overcome, and Psyche was made immortal and united with her lover, bearing him a daughter, Voluptas ("joy").

Psychopompos: *lit.* "the leader," or "conductor of the soul," an epithet of HERMES as conductor of the souls of the deceased to the realms of HADES.

Ptah: ancient Egyptian craftsman and creator god, chief deity of Memphis, the capital during Old Kingdom times (2700–2200 B.C.). His priests regarded him as being the creator of everything, and considered the other great gods to be merely manifestations or aspects of Ptah, who conceived in his heart (i.e. mind) and uttered with his tongue and all things were created. He is represented as human, in mummiform position, wearing the close-fitting skullcap and holding the staff of life, stability and well-being. As divine artificer, he was identified by the Greeks with HEPHAESTUS. The sacred APIS bull of Memphis was regarded as the incarnation of Ptah and OSIRIS. See APIS, SERAPIS.

Pudicitia: *lit.* "modesty," personified Roman goddess of modesty and chastity.

Puranas: a collection of ancient Hindu mythological texts.

Purusha: in Hindu myth, the masculine half of BRAHMA, of whom SATARUPA is the feminine half. In some versions, Purusha is a primeval giant from whose body the universe was created. In the allegorized extension of the concept of Brahma, Purusha is also the universal spirit or world-soul.

Pushan: in Hindu myth, a god of wealth and fertility of cattle, also associated with the sun, guide of travelers and conductor of the souls of the dead.

Pygmalion: legendary king of Cyprus, who fell in love with the ivory statue of a maiden which he had carved, and besought APHRODITE to bring it to life. The goddess answered his prayer, and he married the girl he had fashioned, and she bore him a son named Paphos. Both the islands of Cyprus and Paphos were famous for their many shrines and priestesses of Aphrodite.

Pygmies: in Greek myth, a race of diminutive men dwelling on the borders of Ocean, who every springtime have battle with the cranes. When the cranes attack, the Pygmies advance against them armed with bows and arrows and mounted upon the backs of rams and goats.

Pyrrha: daughter of EPIMETHEUS and wife of DEUCA-LION, with whom she was saved from the flood sent by ZEUS to destroy the degenerate race of mankind.

Pytho (Python): the monster serpent, the offspring of GAIA, or generated from the mud left by the flood of DEUCALION, which infested the region of Parnassus. It was slain by the arrows of APOLLO, who in celebration of the event founded the Pythian Games, and received the epithet of *Pythius*.

Q

Qeb: see GEB

Qebehsenuf: see KEBEHSENUF

Qedesh, Qedeshet: see KEDESH

Quetzalcoatl: among the Indians of Central America, the feathered or plumed serpent-deity, primarily a wind-god, but with attributes widened to include identification with the sun, creation of the world and of man, and instruction of mankind in the nature of the cosmos, the crafts and the arts of civilization.

Quirinus: ancient Latin deity, associated by the Romans with JUPITER and with MARS.

R

Ra (Re), Ra-Atum-Khepri: primal sun-god of ancient Egypt, with whom almost all the local gods were in some way identified even in prehistoric times. He brought himself into being out of the primordial waters, and set in motion the creation of the other gods and everything else in the world. As such, he is called KHEPRI, "he who comes into being, or who brings into being," and is depicted as a scarab-beetle or in human form with a scarab-beetle for a head (because of a pun in the ancient Egyptian language, *kheper* as a verb meaning "to come into being, or bring into being," and as a noun meaning "scarab-beetle"). He is also called ATUM, meaning "he who completes, or perfects," and as such depicted in human form wearing the double crown of Egypt. Ra is also associated with the falcon, and often represented as falcon-headed, this because he was equated with the ancient solar HORUS (not to be confused with Horus, son of ISIS and OSIRIS), and called HER-AKHETY, "Horus of the Two Horizons," or RA-HER-AKHETY.

During the day, Ra sails across the sky in his solar boat, passing under the western horizon at evening and journeying through the underworld, where he is beset by and conquers various malignant adversaries, principally the serpent APEPI, and then rises once more from the eastern horizon.

Ragnarok: *lit.* "the darkness, or twilight, of the gods," in Norse myth the end of the existing universe and of the gods, preceded by struggles and wickedness and by ominous cold and piercing winds. LOKI, FENRIR and the MIDGARD SERPENT will burst their bonds, the forces of HEL will be released, and the monsters and evil powers will fight against the gods. THOR will kill the Midgard Serpent, but will die of its venom. The gods and the evil monsters will be slain, but a new earth will arise, free from all evil. Some of the AESIR, notably VIDAR and VALI, and the sons of Thor will be left alive, as will LIF and LIFTHRASIR of the sons of men, and a new and righteous generation of gods and men will dwell in the world.

Rakshas, Rakshasas: in Hindu myth, evil spirits or demons led by RAVANA.

Rama: in Hindu myth the seventh AVATAR or incarnation of VISHNU, and the hero, with his wife, SITA, of the RAMAYANA epic.

Ramayana: the Hindu epic concerning the adventures of RAMA and his wife SITA, in which Sita is kidnapped by RAVANA, the demon king of Ceylon. With the aid of HANUMAN, the semidivine Monkey King (or his minister), Rama rescues Sita and slays Ravana.

Ran: in Norse myth, the wife of AEGIR, the sea-deity; she drew seafaring men down to herself in the depths.

Rashnu: in ancient Persian myth, one of the YAZATAS and co-judge with MITHRA in the judgment of the dead.

Ravana: in Hindu myth, the ten-headed demon-king of Ceylon, who with his forces of RAKSHASAS kidnaps SITA and after she is rescued by RAMA, is slain by him. See RAMAYANA.

Ravi: in Hindu myth, one of the ADITYAS, guardian deities of the months.

Re: see RA

Remus: see ROMULUS AND REMUS.

Reshef: ancient Syrian name for HADAD, the storm-god.

Rhadamanthus (Rhadamanthys): son of ZEUS and EUROPA, and brother of MINOS, king of Crete, and SARPEDON. Because of his just life on earth, he became one of the three judges of the underworld, together with Minos and AEACUS.

Rhea: one of the early Greek earth and mother goddesses, daughter of OURANOS and GAIA and mate of KRONOS, by whom she became the mother of HERA, HESTIA, DEMETER, HADES, POSEIDON and ZEUS. Kronos, jealous of the future power of his children, devoured each one at birth. When Zeus, the youngest, was born, Rhea deceived Kronos by presenting him with a stone wrapped in swaddling clothes, which he swallowed. She then spirited the infant Zeus away to the Dictaean Cave in Crete, where he was brought up by the KOURETES. As the ancient mother-goddess at Crete, Rhea was identified throughout Classical times with the great mother-goddesses of the ancient Near East, and was also known as RHEA CYBELE and MAGNA MATER ("great mother" of the gods) and was worshipped with orgiastic rites. Like the ancient Near Eastern fertility-goddesses, she is represented upon a lion and with the crescent moon and star of ISHTAR. See CYBELE.

Rhea Silvia: in Roman legend, the VESTAL virgin who became, by MARS, the mother of the twins ROMULUS and REMUS. She was, together with her children, thrown into the Tiber for violating her vow, and Tiberinus, the god of the river, made her his wife.

Rhiannon: in Celtic Welsh myth, "the Great Queen," a mare-goddess comparable to EPONA.

Rig Veda: one of the four groups of the VEDAS, comprising hymns of praise to the gods.

Rimmon: in the Old Testament, a name for the ancient Near Eastern storm-god HADAD.

Rishis: in Hindu myth, the legendary seven seers and/or sages of mythic times, frequently connected with the PRAJAPATIS.

Romulus and Remus: the twin sons of RHEA SILVIA by MARS. Their mother being a VESTAL, they were ordered to be thrown into the Tiber and drowned, but were miraculously saved and reared by a she-wolf together with her cubs. When they grew up, Romulus slew Remus in a quarrel and later founded the city of Rome, which he named after himself, becoming its first king. After his death he was deified. According to another, possibly older version, the twins were the children of Ilia, daughter of AENEAS and Lavinia, the native Latin princess Aeneas had married.

Rudra: *lit.* "the ruddy one"; in Hindu myth a god of thunder and storm, later becoming partially identified with SHIVA.

S

Sabazios: in late Classical times, a deity originating in Phrygian Asia Minor, frequently identified with DIONYSUS and with ZEUS and associated in his mystery cult with them and with CYBELE. As his cult spread during the time of the Roman Empire, he was by some identified with YAHWEH *Sabaoth* of the Old Testament. His chief attributive symbol is the serpent, indicating his basically paternal and phallic nature.

Saga: in Norse myth, believed to be a goddess who knows all things, hence a goddess of the poetic arts and history.

Sakti: see SHAKTI

Salacia: Roman goddess of the salt sea (*sal,* "salt"). She was identified with AMPHITRITE, and hence was wife of NEPTUNE (POSEIDON).

Salmacis: the nymph of the spring of that name near Halicarnassus in Asia Minor. She loved HERMAPHRODITUS, the beautiful son of HERMES and APHRODITE, and was granted her request to be united in the same body with him. Hence the dual sexuality of Hermaphroditus and the legend that the spring Salmacis rendered effeminate those who bathed in or drank of its waters.

Salmoneus: legendary Greek king, son of AEOLUS and brother of SISYPHUS. He attempted to usurp the name and prerogatives of ZEUS, ordering sacrifices to himself and producing imitation thunder and lightning by trailing dried skins and cauldrons behind his chariot and flinging flaming torches into the air. For this, Zeus slew him with his thunderbolt and destroyed his city.

Salus: personified Roman goddess of health, prosperity and the public welfare.

Sama Veda: one of the four groups of the VEDAS, consisting of ceremonies of the SOMA.

Sancus: ancient Roman deity presiding over oaths and good faith.

Saranyu: in Hindu myth, wife of SURYA, the sun-god, and sometimes regarded as a dawn-goddess.

Sarasvati: in Hindu myth, a goddess of the river waters and of fertility and wealth, consort of BRAHMA and patroness of speech, writing and learning, and of the arts and sciences.

Sarpanit: see ZARPANIT

Sarpedon: son of ZEUS and EUROPA, and brother of MINOS and RHADAMANTHUS. Like his brothers, he was a favorite of the gods, and Zeus granted him the privilege of living for three (or six) generations. He was an ally of Troy during the Trojan War, and was slain by PATROCLUS.

Satan: *lit.* "the adversary," found personified only in the late prologue and epilogue to the Book of Job in the Old Testament, and translated into Greek as *diabolos,* "adversary, prosecutor," whence is derived the English word *devil.* In medieval Judeo-Christian theology the term was applied to the personified conception of the chief of the angels, the jealous enemy of mankind who rebelled and was

cast down into Hell, becoming lord of that region
and constant tempter and seducer of men, in order
to entrap them into his power and inflict punishment upon them after death.

Saturnus (Saturn): Roman name of KRONOS.

Satyrs: Greek woodland deities representing the lux-
uriant vital powers of fertility and wild nature,
usually represented with pointed ears, goat's horns
and erect phalli. They are fond of wine and all the
sexual pleasures, and are the masculine counterparts of the NYMPHS. Dancing wildly and carrying
the *thyrsus,* they are constantly in the train of
DIONYSUS, and associated with his worship.

Savitri, Savitar: in Hindu myth, one of the ADITYAS,
guardian deities of the months. He is primarily a
sun-god, and evidently the same as SURYA.

Scarabaeus: the scarab-beetle, a symbol and embodiment of the Egyptian god RA as KHEPRI, which see.

Scylla and **Charybdis:** female monsters dwelling in
caves within two perilous rocks in the Straits of
Messina between Italy and Sicily. Scylla has twelve
feet, six necks, and six heads each having three
rows of sharp teeth, and barks like a dog. If a ship
comes too close, she snatches up one of the men
with each of her heads, as she did to the crew of
ODYSSEUS. Charybdis's cave has a huge fig tree growing over it, and thrice every day she swallows all
the waters of the sea and spews them up again,
forming a terrible whirlpool. Whoever tries to
avoid one of the two disasters falls prey to the
other.

Seb: older and erroneous rendering of GEB.

Sebek: ancient Egyptian crocodile god, sometimes

identified with RA or with SET, and regarded as the son of NEITH.

Seker (Sokar): one of the gods of the afterworld in ancient Egypt, venerated mostly in the funerary ritual at Memphis, and often identified with PTAH and OSIRIS. He is usually represented in mummiform human shape, with a falcon's head and an elaborate crown.

Sekhmet: *lit.* "the powerful one," ancient Egyptian goddess with the head of a lioness, the consort of PTAH and by him mother of NEFERTEM, comprising the triad of Memphis. She is a fierce goddess of destruction and war, similar to the destructive aspect of HATHOR. Because of her feline head, she was in the late period sometimes confused with BASTET (BAST).

Selene: Greek goddess of the moon, daughter of HYPERION and sister of HELIOS (the Sun) and EOS (the Dawn). She fell in love with the beautiful shepherd ENDYMION, and caused him to sleep so that she might caress him undisturbed.

Selket (Selkit, Serket): ancient Egyptian scorpiongoddess, represented as a woman with a scorpion on her head; one of the goddesses, with ISIS, NEPHTHYS and NEITH, who guards the CANOPIC JARS containing the entrails of the deceased.

Semele: daughter of CADMUS king of Thebes, and sister of INO and AGAVE. She was beloved by ZEUS, and at the jealous instigation of HERA, forced him to appear before her in all his splendor. Zeus appeared to her with thunder and lightning, and Semele was consumed in the flames. Zeus, however, snatched her unborn child by him from her body and sewed it into his own thigh, whence it was later born as

DIONYSUS. Dionysus later conducted her out of Hades to Olympus and made her immortal.

Semiramis: in Classical literature, a legendary queen of Assyria, daughter of ATARGATIS or DERCETO. She was famed for her beauty, intelligence and sensuality, and reputed to have built the city of Babylon, among others.

Seraphim: term used in the Old Testament designating certain divine creatures associated with the CHERUBIM, and later taken to be angels. The word means "the fiery, or burning ones" in Hebrew and they are described as winged. Possibly they were originally legendary winged serpents.

Serapis: the state god of Egypt during the times of the Ptolemies. The name is a Greek version of a combination of OSIRIS and APIS, the sacred bull which was regarded as the incarnation of PTAH. Serapis is represented in typically Greek style, as a man with thick curly hair and beard, similar to ZEUS, with a basket or cuplike vessel upon his head.

Serket: see SELKET

Set (Setekh, Setesh, Seth): ancient Egyptian fertility-god, and deity of storm and turmoil, son of GEB and NUT and brother of OSIRIS, ISIS and NEPHTHYS, the latter sometimes mentioned as his consort. In historical times he was the "villain" among the gods (see OSIRIS), but always worshipped as a powerful deity to be propitiated. As antagonist of the great gods Osiris and HORUS, he was equated by the Greeks with the serpent TYPHON, as the Egyptians themselves sometimes equated him with APEPI. Because of his storm and fertility aspects, the Egyptians also identified him with the Canaanite god BAAL. He is depicted as a peculiar doglike animal with a curved snout and erect ears with square ends, sitting on his haunches, or in human form with the head of that animal. The animal itself has been variously thought to be a species of dog, an ass, a pig or some wild beast like the okapi, but its exact identification remains obscure.

Shakti, Sakti: in Hindu myth, the appellation of the consort of SHIVA as the female principle of active, dynamic potency.

Shaman: magician and "medicine man" among the northern Siberian and Eskimo tribes. The shaman operates by means of ecstasy, into which he excites himself by means of his drum, and in this state of trance leaves his body and communes with the spirits for purposes of divination.

Shamash: ancient Sumero-Babylonian sun-god, represented as rising from or striding upon the mountains, with rays issuing from his shoulders. He was regarded as upholder of truth and justice, and together with SIN and HADAD (or ADAD) he makes up the second triad of Mesopotamian gods. In the Sumerian texts, he is known as UTU or BAB-BAR.

Shang-Ti: in Chinese myth, the supreme ancestor-god, originally a chthonic vegetation-deity. He is regarded as Lord of Heaven (TIEN), and often referred to by that name.

Shasti: in Hindu myth, a protective goddess of children.

Shen Nung: in Chinese myth, an early legendary emperor who taught his people the arts of agriculture and was later elevated to deity.

Sheol: in the Old Testament, a dim region under the

earth, where the spirits of all the deceased wander about as pale shades.

Shesanaga: in Hindu myth, the great serpent which lies on the primordial Ocean of Milk, and upon whom reclines NARAYANA (or VISHNU). He is also regarded as king of the NAGAS, or serpent-people, and has a thousand heads.

Shichi Fukujin: in Japanese myth, the seven deities of good fortune, one goddess and six gods: Bentne, Bishamon, Daikoku, Ebisu, Fukurokuju, Hotei and Jurojin.

Shinto: the official religion of imperial Japan, called "the way of the gods" and centering about the worship of the emperor as decended from IZANAGI, with a multiplicity of ancestral deities added to intrench the status of the military caste.

Shiva: in Hindu myth, the third deity of the TRI-MURTI, or triad of great gods. He is called the Destroyer, but has also the aspect of regeneration. As destroyer, he is dark and terrible, appearing as a naked ascetic accompanied by a train of hideous demons, encircled with serpents and necklaces of skulls. As auspicious and reproductive power, he is worshipped in the form of the LINGA, or phallus. He is depicted as white, with a dark-blue throat, with several arms and three eyes, carrying a trident and riding on a white bull. His consort is PARVATI (DEVI).

Shu: personified god of the air in ancient Egypt, who, together with TEFNUT ("moisture"), was produced by the creator and sun-god RA from his own body by masturbation. Shu and Tefnut then mated, and the ensuing generations of the gods proceeded from them. Shu is frequently depicted symbolically holding up the sky-goddess NUT, who is stretched over the earth.

Sibylline Books: a collection of nine books of prophecies regarding the future destinies of Rome, and bought from the CUMAEAN SIBYL by TARQUIN. When she offered to sell him all nine books he refused to pay the price she asked, whereupon she burned three of them and offered the rest for the original price. When he refused, she burned three more, offering the remaining three again for the original price. At this, his estimation of their value increased and he bought the three books for the price at which he could have bought all nine. They were kept at Rome in the Capitol, which was destroyed by fire in 83 B.C. A new collection was prepared and during the centuries (until 405 A.D. when it was burned) additional, later matter was added, from Jewish and Christian sources. Some of this material has survived.

Sibyls: a series of prophetesses of the early days of Rome. The first of these was the CUMAEAN SIBYL, who was said to have come from the East.

Sid: (pronounced *shee*) in Celtic myth, the hidden world which is the dwelling of the divinities and other supernatural beings. Sids are located beneath the earth, within hills, beneath the ocean, and at the mysterious, unknown frontiers of the world.

Siegfried: see SIGURD

Sigurd, Siegfried: the hero of the Norse saga of the Treasure of the NIFLUNGS (NIBLUNGS). He slew the dragon FAFNIR and loved the princess BRYNHILD, but forgot her after drinking the magic potion offered him by GRIMHILD, so that he married the latter's daughter GUDRUN. He was later treacherously slain through the plotting of Gudrun's brothers GUNNAR and HOGNI.

Silenus: originally plural (*Sileni*) spirits of wild nature like the SATYRS. Later mentioned as one Silenus, who was the tutor and constant companion of the young DIONYSUS. Silenus is usually represented as a plump, jovial old man with a long beard and generally drunk. He has much wisdom, however, and if captured by mortals can reveal important secrets. He is often mentioned as the father of the Satyrs.

Silvanus: ancient Latin divinity of wild fields, forests and groves and presiding over boundaries. As fertility god he is protector of herds and cattle and associated with PAN, FAUNUS, etc.

Sin: ancient Sumero-Babylonian moon-god, sometimes regarded as the son of ENLIL. He is lord of the calendar, fixing the seasons, and also a vegetation-deity and patron of fertility. With SHAMASH and HADAD (or ADAD) he makes up the second triad of Mesopotamian gods.

Sina (Hina, Ina): the moon-goddess in Polynesian myth, and consort of MAUI. The resemblance of her name to that of SIN is interesting, but one must beware of hasty conclusions not founded on factual evidence. This applies, of course, to the entire study of myth and comparative religion and to the human behavioral sciences in general.

Sirens: ancient Greek sea-nymphs who by the irrestible charm of their song lured mariners to their destruction on the rocks surrounding their island. ODYSSEUS escaped them by stuffing his companions' ears with wax and having himself lashed to the mast of his ship.

Sisyphus: son of AEOLUS, brother of SALMONEUS and founder and king of the city of Corinth. Because of his avarice and fraudulence, he was condemned, in the lower world, eternally to roll a block of stone to the top of a steep hill, whence it always rolled down to the bottom again.

Sita: in Hindu myth, the wife of RAMA, who was kidnapped by RAVANA. As Rama was an incarnation of VISHNU, so Sita was an incarnation of LAKSHMI or SRI. In the VEDAS, Sita is "the Furrow," the personified goddess of the female principle and fertility.

Siva: see SHIVA

Skambha: in Hindu myth, an appellation of PURUSHA as the masculine half of BRAHMA, "a vast embodied being coextensive with the universe."

Skuld: in Norse myth, one of the NORNS, which see.

Sokar: see SEKER

Sol: Latin word for "sun," and god of the sun when personified. See HELIOS.

Soma: in Hindu myth, the personified deity of the fermented juice of a legendary plant which was drunk by gods and men to produce a state of intoxicating ecstasy. The soma juice was believed to confer inward fire and immortality, and was also associated with the moon. In the hymns of the ZEND AVESTA it is called HAOMA.

Somnus: personified Roman god of sleep, a translation of the Greek HYPNOS.

Spes: *lit.* "hope" in Latin, personified Roman goddess of that name.

Sphinx: in Greek myth, a legendary winged monster, with the body of a lion and the head and breasts of a woman, the offspring of TYPHON and ECHIDNA. She placed herself on a high rock near Thebes, and posed a riddle to all who passed, and killed those who could not answer. The riddle was: "What has four feet, two feet and three feet, but one voice?" When OEDIPUS answered that it was Man, who first crawls on all fours, then walks on his two legs and when old uses a staff to help him walk, the Sphinx threw herself headlong down the rock. The so-called Great Sphinx in Egypt is not a sphinx at all, but a representation of the head of Khaf-Ra (Cephren), an early king of Egypt, on the body of a crouching lion. The name "sphinx" was applied to those rather common lion-bodied portraits of the Egyptian kings by the Greeks who visited the country during the later period, because of the general similarity of these statues to their legendary Sphinx.

Sraosha: in ancient Persian myth, one of the YAZATAS who bears the souls of the dead to Paradise.

Sri: in Hindu myth, one of the appellations of LAKSH-MI, goddess of beauty and good fortune.

Sterope: one of the seven nymphs, daughters of ATLAS, who constitute the PLEIADES.

Sthenno: one of the three GORGONS.

Styx: the mythical river which flows seven times around the realms of HADES. As the personified spirit of the river, she was the first who aided ZEUS against the TITANS, and in reward was appointed the divinity by whom the gods swore their inviolable oaths.

Summanus: ancient Etruscan deity, regarded by the Romans as the nocturnal counterpart of JUPITER, hurling his thunderbolts by night as Jupiter did by day.

Surya: in Hindu myth, one of the ADITYAS, guardian deities of the months, and god of the sun, dwelling in its body.

Sut, Sutesh: see SET

Syrinx: a river-nymph of Arcadia in Greece, who was pursued by PAN and fled into the waters of her river, where she was changed into a reed. Pan cut the reed into pieces of gradually decreasing lengths, fastened them together with wax and thus produced the shepherd's flute, or "pipes of Pan," upon which he plays.

T

Tahuti (or **Tehuti**) : one form of transliteration of the name of the ancient Egyptian god better known as THOTH (the Greek version of the name).

Talisman: an apotropaic, or protective, charm of metal or stone, often bearing a magic formula or device and carried on one's person as protection against malignant influences.

Tammuz: ancient Sumero-Babylonian fertility-god, described as the son, brother and beloved of the goddess ISHTAR. He is slain and descends to the nether world, and woe and desolation fall upon the earth. Ishtar leads the world in lamentation and then descends to the nether world, which is ruled by the dark and violent goddess ERESHKIGAL, and after many trials succeeds in bringing Tammuz back, as a result of which fertility and joy return to the earth. In ancient Syria, he was identified with ADONIS.

Tanith: mother and fertility goddess of Phoenician Carthage, consort of the Carthaginian BAAL whom the Romans identified with KRONOS.

Tantalus: son of ZEUS and father of PELOPS and NIOBE. He is famous for the punishment meted out to him after his death. He was placed in a pool of water and afflicted with a raging thirst, but the waters receded whenever he attempted to drink. Over his head hung branches of fruit, which sprang out of his reach whenever he attempted to reach it; hence the word *tantalize*. His crime is variously given as that of attempting to test the gods by serving them the boiled flesh of his son Pelops at a banquet, that of divulging the secrets entrusted to him by Zeus, or that of stealing nectar and ambrosia from the table of the gods.

Taranis: thunder-god of ancient Gaul, whom the Romans described as receiving human sacrifices.

Taouris (or Taourt): in ancient Egyptian, *ta-weret*, "the great one." Egyptian goddess of pregnancy and birth, represented as a female hippopotamus with a huge belly, standing upright on her hind legs.

Taraka: in Hindu myth, the demon-king who was slain by KARTIKEYA.

Tarquin: Tarquinius Superbus, one of the early kings of Rome, who was reputed to have bought the SIBYLLINE BOOKS. Although he was a tyrannical ruler, he brought Rome to a height of power and influence. The events leading to his downfall began when one of his sons forcibly violated LUCRETIA, his cousin's wife.

Tartarus: son of AITHER and GE (GAIA) and, by his own mother, the father of TYPHOEUS and ECHIDNA. Possibly by association, Tartarus came to denote the dark abyss beneath the domains of HADES where the rebellious TITANS and other heinous offenders were punished. It was as far beneath the surface of the earth as the earth is beneath the heavens.

Tefnut: ancient Egyptian personified goddess of moisture, together with the consort SHU (Air) produced by RA from his own body by masturbation. By Shu, Tefnut became the mother of GEB (Earth) and NUT (Sky).

Tehuti, Tahuti: see THOTH

Telchines: in Greek myth, legendary primitive tribe represented as early cultivators of the soil, ministers of the gods and inventors of the useful arts, working in bronze and iron. They were also regarded as sorcerers and envious demons with the power of controlling the destructive elements.

Telegonus: son of ODYSSEUS and CIRCE, sent by his mother to follow after his father. He was shipwrecked on the coast of Ithaca, and driven by hunger, he ravaged the fields. When Odysseus and TELEMACHUS came to fight against him he ran his father through with his spear, not knowing who he was. At ATHENA's command, Telegonus, Telemachus and PENELOPE buried the body of Odysseus on Circe's island, where Telegonus married Penelope.

Telemachus: son of ODYSSEUS and PENELOPE. He was an infant when his father left for Troy, and when his father had not yet returned after twenty years, he went in search of him. He eventually came to Sparta and met MENELAOS, who told him of a prophecy concerning his father's homecoming. He then returned home to Ithaca, where he found his father.

Tellus: *lit.* "the earth, the world," as personification of the ancient Roman mother and fertility goddess, and known as the BONA DEA.

Tem, Temu, Tum: variation of *Atum*, an aspect of the ancient Egyptian god RA, which see.

Tenjin: Japanese god of learning and calligraphy.

Teraphim: the little images of ancient Syrian household gods mentioned in the Old Testament in connection with the story of Rachel. They probably corresponded to the Roman ancestral LARES and PENATES.

Terminus: ancient Roman deity protecting boundaries and frontiers, developed from the rude stone markers which were consecrated and at which ritual offerings were made.

Terpsichore: Greek Muse of the choral dance and song, usually represented with the lyre. See MUSES.

Terra: "the Earth" as personification of the ancient Roman mother and fertility goddess, known as the BONA DEA.

Teshub: ancient Hittite name for HADAD, the storm-god.

Tethra: in Celtic myth, a divine king of the FORMORIANS, who reigns over the creatures of the sea, "the herds of Tethra."

Tethys: daughter of OURANOS and GAIA, and wife of OCEANUS, by whom she became the mother of the sea-nymphs, the OCEANIDES.

Tetragrammaton: Greek word meaning "the four-letter (word)"; the four Hebrew consonants, *Yhwh,* of the name of the Deity as given in the Old Testament (YAHWEH).

Teutates: *lit.* "the god of the tribe," ancient Celtic deity equated by the Romans with MARS, and to whom human sacrifices were offered.

Tezcatlipoca: *lit.* "smoking mirror," chief god of the Aztecs, identified with the obsidian knife-god, and the deity who commanded the Aztec Noah to build a ship in order to save himself from the Flood.

Thalia: Greek Muse of comedy, usually represented with comic mask and/or shepherd's staff (see MUSES). Thalia was also the name of one of the GRACES, or CHARITES.

Thanatos: personified Greek god of death, son of NOX (NYX) and twin brother of HYPNOS (Sleep), and dwelling in the lower world.

Thaumas: *lit.* "wonder," son of GAIA and father of IRIS, the rainbow-goddess.

Themis: a daughter of OURANOS and GAIA, she personifies the divine right order of things as sanctioned by custom and law. As such she is also the original goddess of prophecy, revealing what must of necessity occur, and received the oracle of Delphi from her mother Gaia, later transmitting it to APOLLO.

Theseus: legendary hero and later king of Athens, son of AEGAEUS (or the god POSEIDON). During his adventurous youth, he rid Attica of various terrible evildoers and monsters, and volunteered to go to Crete with the tribute of seven youths and seven maidens which the Athenians were obliged to send as tribute to be devoured by the MINOTAUR. With the aid of ARIADNE, daughter of King MINOS of Crete, he slew the Minotaur and escaped with his companions, taking Ariadne with him, only to abandon her on the island of Naxos. His other adventures entailed a battle with the AMAZONS, by whose queen ANTIOPE (or HIPPOLYTE) he had a son, HIPPOLYTUS, and later married PHAEDRA, younger daughter of Minos. With the assistance of his friend Pirithoüs, he carried HELEN off from Sparta when she was a girl, and aided Pirithoüs in his attempt to abduct PERSEPHONE from Hades.

Thetis: one of the NEREIDS. Her affections were sought by ZEUS, but when the latter was told of the prophecy of THEMIS that Thetis's son would become more powerful than his father, he married her to PELEUS. By Peleus she became the mother of ACHILLES.

Thor: in Norse myth, son of ODIN and a god of fertility and especially of thunder and lightning produced by the goat-drawn chariot in which he rides. He is also the chief protagonist of gods and men in the battle against the Giants, whom he fights with his huge hammer which always finds its mark and always returns to his hand.

Thoth (Tehuti, Tahuti): Greek rendering of

Djehuti, the name of the ancient Egyptian god of writing and patron deity of knowledge and the sciences in general, the inventor of the hieroglyphic system of writing and of numbers, geometry, etc. Hence he was the scribe of the gods, the attorney before the divine council and the repository of the various magic formulae which are necessary in this world and the next. Thus one of his important functions was that of recorder at the scene of the judgment of the deceased before OSIRIS. He was also associated with the moon, and was probably a moon-god in earliest times. He was usually represented as a man with the head of an ibis, which bird was sacred to him, as well as the cynocephalus, or dog-headed ape.

Thule: in Classical myth, the legendary island situated in the extreme north sea, regarded as the northernmost, or extreme point on the earth (*Ultima Thule*).

Thyestes: son of PELOPS and brother of ATREUS. As result of a quarrel with Atreus, the latter killed the two sons of Thyestes and served him their flesh at a banquet. Thyestes fled in horror, and the gods cursed Atreus and his house. By his own daughter Pelopia, he became the father of AEGISTHUS, who later murdered Atreus's son AGAMEMNON.

Tiamat: primeval Sumero-Babylonian goddess personifying the primordial salt-water ocean, the waters of CHAOS. She is described as a huge, bloated dragon-monster whose consort is APSU, the abyss of sweet waters under the earth. From Tiamat and Apsu proceeded the ensuing generations of the gods. She was later slain by MARDUK, who split her body in two, fixing one half of it on high to become the watery vault of the heavens. "The deep" (Hebrew *tehom*) at the beginning of Genesis derives from Tiamat.

Tien: Heaven in Chinese belief, or the appellation of SHANG-TI, the supreme ancestral god who is its ruler.

Tiresias: celebrated blind prophet of Thebes, who played a prominent role in many of the ancient Greek myths, and was consulted by ODYSSEUS, who brought him up from the shades of the dead for the purpose. Various reasons are given for his blindness, among them being that he was made so by ATHENA, whom he had come upon while she was bathing naked, and that in remorse she gave him the gift of prophecy. According to another tradition, he was the only mortal who had been both male and female, as a result of having killed first the female of a pair of coupling serpents and seven years later the male of another pair. He was therefore called in to decide the issue of an argument between ZEUS and HERA as to which sex derives the most pleasure from the sexual act, Hera maintaining that the man does. Tiresias replied that the woman derives nine times as much pleasure as the man, whereupon Hera struck him with blindness. In compensation, Zeus bestowed upon him the gift of prophecy.

Tisiphone: one of the three FURIES.

Tistrya, Tishtrya: in ancient Persian myth, the personified deity of Sirius the Dog Star and helper of AHRIMAN against AHURA-MAZDA.

Titania: in some medieval folklore, the queen of the fairies, OBERON being the king.

Titans: the offspring of OURANOS and GAIA. They were twelve deities—six male: OCEANUS, HYPERION, Coeus, KRONOS, Krios, and IAPETUS, and six female: TETHYS, Theia, PHOEBE, RHEA, THEMIS and MNEMOSYNE. They were incited to rebel against and castrate their father by Gaia, and the deed was carried out by Kronos. The best known are Kronos and Rhea who became the parents of the Olympian deities and Mnemosyne (Memory) who became the mother of the MUSES by ZEUS. Their children and grandchildren are often also referred to as Titans.

Tithonus: son of LAOMEDON, king of Troy, and brother of PRIAM. He was beloved of EOS, goddess of the dawn, who obtained the gift of immortality for him, from the gods, neglecting to ask for eternal youth also. As a result, he grew extremely old and decrepit and, by some accounts, was finally changed into a grasshopper.

Tlaloc: Aztec rain-god to whom numbers of children were sacrificed every year by drowning.

Tlazolteotl: earth and mother goddess of the Aztecs and goddess of dirt, lust and sexual sin.

Torah: *lit.* "the teaching" (i.e. of Moses), the name of the first section of the Hebrew Bible, consisting of the Five Books of Moses (the *Pentateuch*).

Trimurti: the triad of the great Hindu gods which proceeded from the world-egg deposited by the supreme First Cause: BRAHMA, the Creator; VISHNU, the Preserver; and SHIVA, the Destroyer.

Triptolemos: son of CELEUS, king of Eleusis (near Athens), and his queen METANEIRA. DEMETER, while wandering in search of her daughter PERSEPHONE, was hospitably received by Celeus. In gratitude, she secretly attempted to make Triptolemos immortal by purifying him in the fire, but was discovered by his mother, who was hysterically alarmed at the sight. In some earlier versions of the myth, this son of Celeus is Demophoön, and Triptolemos is Demophoön's brother. Demeter sent Triptolemos over the earth in a chariot drawn by winged serpents to teach mankind the arts of agriculture. On his return, his father Celeus attempted to kill him, but at Demeter's command he was forced to desist and to yield up his kingdom to Triptolemos. Triptolemos founded the Eleusinian Mysteries in honor of Demeter, in the rituals of which the myth was no doubt re-enacted.

Trismegistus: see HERMES TRISMEGISTUS

Triton: son of POSEIDON and AMPHITRITE, living with them in a golden palace in the depths of the sea. Triton is represented as having the body of a man with the tail of a fish or a dolphin (i.e. a "merman"), and sometimes has the forefeet of a horse in addition. He carries a twisted conch shell, upon which he blows either violently or gently, to stir up or to calm the waves. In later times a multiplicity of Tritons was imagined, as attending the various divinities associated with the sea.

Trivia: personified Roman deity of crossroads, from the Latin *trivium*, "meeting of three roads." She was represented with three faces, and sometimes identified with HECATE.

Trophonius: and Agamedes, sons of a legendary king of Orchomenos in Greece, became famous as architects, and constructed, among other buildings, the temple of APOLLO at Delphi and a royal treasury in Boeotia. In the wall of the latter they inserted a stone which could easily be removed, and so systematically robbed the treasury by night. The king, however, set traps within, and one night Agamedes was caught. Trophonius then cut off his brother's head to prevent his being betrayed as his accomplice. He was pursued by the king nevertheless, but was swallowed up by the earth in the grove of Lebadea. There he was worshipped as a hero and by command of Apollo the subterranean "Cave of Trophonius" became the seat of an oracle. The descent into the cave and the awe-inspiring sights there were so terrifying that it was believed that anyone who descended into the Cave of Trophonius never smiled again.

Tsuki-Yumi: Japanese moon-god and brother of the sun-goddess AMA-TERASU, which see.

Tuamutef: see DUAMUTEF

Tuatha De Danann: *lit.* "the tribes of the goddess DANA," in Celtic myth one of the divine prehistoric peoples of Ireland, skilled in magic and in all the arts and crafts, and also powerful warriors.

Tum, Temu: variation of ATUM, an aspect of the ancient Egyptian god RA, which see.

Tvashtri, Tvashtar: in Hindu myth, the artificer of the gods who forged the thunderbolt of INDRA and the cup for the divine SOMA.

Tyche: Greek goddess, originally of fortune and chance, and then of prosperity, having cities under her special protection. In later times, each city was considered to have its special Tyche. The Romans identified her with the early Italian goddess FORTUNA.

Tyndareus: legendary king of Sparta and husband of

LEDA, who became the mother of CASTOR, POLLUX, HELEN and CLYTEMNESTRA. According to one tradition Leda, who was loved by ZEUS in the form of a swan, laid an egg in which were all four children. Another tradition had it that Leda was embraced by both Zeus and Tyndareus during the same night, and that Pollux and Helen were the children of Zeus and born from the egg, while Castor and Clytemnestra were the children of Tyndareus.

Typhon (Typhaon, Typhoeus): a huge dragonlike monster, with a hundred snake-heads, the offspring of GAIA and TARTARUS. He was associated with the turmoil and storm of the wind and the sea, and is described as contending with ZEUS himself, or with APOLLO. He was confined in Tartarus, or lies buried beneath Mt. Aetna. By ECHIDNA he was the father of the SPHINX. Later Greek writers on Egypt identified him with the Egyptian "evil" god SET.

Tyr: in Norse myth, son of ODIN and a daughter of one of the primeval giants, the boldest of the gods, who inspires courage and heroism in battle. He was the only one who dared to feed FENRIR (the FENRIS wolf), who bit off one of his hands.

U

Ukemochi: Japanese food and fertility-goddess, whose attributes are often absorbed into those of INARI.

Ulysses: from the Latin *Ulixes*, Roman name for ODYSSEUS.

Uma: in Hindu myth, one of the appellations of PARVATI (DEVI) as "light" or "splendor," embodying great beauty and divine wisdom.

Undines: in Teutonic folklore, a group of water-nymphs or mermaids, who liked to associate with humans and join them in their village dances.

Upanishads: a series of Hindu sacred texts, philosophical commentaries to the VEDAS.

Upis: a surname or epithet of ARTEMIS as tutelary goddess of childbirth, sometimes mentioned as the nymph who reared her, or even in masculine form as the father of Artemis.

Urania: Greek Muse of astronomy, usually represented with a globe. See MUSES.

Uranus: see OURANOS

Urd: in Norse myth, one of the NORNS, which see.

Uroboros: see OUROBOROS

Ushas: in Hindu myth, the goddess of the dawn and in the VEDAS the breath of life.

Utgard: in Norse myth, the chief city of JOTUN-HEIM, the abode of the Giants.

Utnapishtim: the "Babylonian Noah" of ancient Mesopotamian myth. As related in the GILGAMESH EPIC, the gods secretly decided to destroy mankind by a flood, but the god EA (ENKI), who was friendly to man, passed the plan on to Utnapishtim, instructing him to build a boat in which he was to gather his family, his possessions and all kinds of cattle and wild animals. He did so, and then the rains began and lasted for seven days, destroying all living creatures. The boat rested on Mt. Nisir, and Utnapishtim released in succession a dove, a swallow and a raven. The raven did not return, and Utnapishtim, thus knowing that the waters had subsided, opened the boat and then offered grateful sacrifice to the gods. For his piety, Utnapishtim and his wife were granted immortality.

Utu: ancient Sumerian sun-god, corresponding to the Babylonian SHAMASH.

Uzza: *lit.* "the migthy one," pre-Islamic Arabian goddess personifying the planet Venus and worshipped in the form of an acacia tree.

V

Vach: in Hindu myth, the goddess of speech and eloquence, and the mother of the VEDAS. She was later identified with SARASVATI.

Valhalla: in Norse myth, the banquet hall of the AESIR in ASGARD, where the slain warriors feasted and rejoiced in immortality.

Vali: in Norse myth, a son of ODIN who will be left alive after RAGNAROK.

Valkyries: in Norse myth, the "Maidens of ODIN," who rode through the air in full armor and who assigned victory to warriors and chose those to be slain, bearing them off to VALHALLA.

Vanaheim: in Norse myth, the dwelling of the VANIR.

Vanir: in Norse myth, a group of deities of wild nature and fertility.

Var, Vara: in ancient Persian myth, the cave in which YIMA took refuge from the Flood.

Varuna: in Hindu myth, one of the ADITYAS, guardian deities of the months, god of the waters and/ or the heavens and of the west.

Vasuki: in Hindu myth, a king of the NAGAS, similar to SESHA.

Vayu: in Hindu myth, an early deity of the wind, or wind-spirit.

Ve: in Norse myth, brother of ODIN and VILI and son of BORR.

Vedas: the most ancient sacred texts of the Hindus. There are four groups of these texts: The RIG VEDA, comprising hymns of praise to the gods; the YAJUR VEDA, consisting of sacrificial texts; the SAMA VEDA, dealing with SOMA ceremonies; and the ARTARVA VEDA, comprising magical spells.

Venus: Roman goddess corresponding to APHRODITE.

Verdandi: in Norse myth, one of the NORNS, which see.

Vertumnus: ancient Latin deity of seasons, changes and ripening of plant life, and hence associated with the fruit-goddess POMONA.

Vesta: Roman name of HESTIA.

Vestals: the priestesses of the Roman VESTA, who was the Greek HESTIA. The Vestals' sacred duty was to tend the eternal fire of Vesta in her temple, and for the thirty years of their service they had to remain virgins like the goddess. The penalty for their violation of virginity was burial alive.

Victoria: personified Roman goddess of victory, as the Greek NIKE.

Vidar, Vidur: in Norse myth, a son of ODIN and a giantess, and after THOR the strongest of the gods. At RAGNAROK he will cleave the throat of FENRIR with his thick boot. He is also known as "the god of few words."

Vili: in Norse myth, brother of ODIN and VE and son of BORR.

Virabhadra: in Hindu myth, a monster created by SHIVA in his quarrel with DAKSHA.

Vishnu: in Hindu myth, the second deity of the TRI-MURTI, or triad of the great gods. His function is preservation, and he pervades all things. Among his followers he is the Supreme Living Spirit, and as such often identified with NARAYANA and shown reclining on the serpent SHESANAGA on the primordial Ocean of Milk while BRAHMA issues from a lotus growing from his navel. Periodically he descends to earth in the form of an AVATAR, or incarnation, to deliver mankind from great perils. The number of avatars is usually given as ten, the last of which was the ninth, *Gautama* BUDDHA, and the tenth, KALKI, is yet to come. His consort is LAKSHMI.

Visvakarma: a form of VIVASVAT, which see.

Vivasvat: in Hindu myth the sun as divinity, also regarded as the architect who built the cities of the gods.

Voltumna: ancient Latin goddess, a feminine form of VERTUMNUS.

Voluspa: "the song of the prophetess," one of the texts of the EDDAS, in which is narrated the events of RAGNAROK.

Vrihaspati: in Hindu myth, the preceptor of the gods and guardian of hymns and prayers.

Vritra: in Hindu myth a dragon-deity, often identified with AHI, who withheld and guarded the fructifying waters, causing drought, until he was slain by INDRA.

Vulcan: Roman deity of fire and craftsmanship, identified with the Greek god HEPHAESTOS.

Vulturnus: Latin name for the Greek EURUS, god of the East Wind.

W

Waukheon: "the Thunderbird," god of the thunder-cloud among the Dakota Indians, who is constantly fighting with the water-god.

Wen-Chang: Chinese god of literature, invoked by scholars to assist them in their labors, and believed to reside in the constellation of the Great Bear.

Woden, Wodin, Wotan: Teutonic rendering of the Norse ODIN, which see.

X

Xibalba: in Mayan myth, the realm of the evil demons who challenged the gods to combat.

Xilonen: Aztec maize-goddess, called "the hairy mother" possibly with reference to the hairlike tassels of the corn. Human sacrifices were made to her at midsummer.

Xipe: Aztec god called "Our Lord the Flayed One," represented clothed in a human skin from the body of a flayed captive sacrificed to him.

Xochiquetzal: *lit.* "flower-feather," Aztec goddess of flowers and love and patroness-deity of prostitutes. She was also patroness of the crafts.

Y

Yaaru: in ancient Egyptian belief, the fields in the nether-world domains of OSIRIS, which were tilled to provide the dead with food, and analogous to the ELYSIAN FIELDS of the Greeks.

Yahweh (or **Yahveh, Jahveh,** etc.): The name of the Deity, as given in the Old Testament. In the Hebrew, it means "He who causes to come into existence." The name was later considered too sacred to pronounce, and at every occurrence of the name, the word *Adonai* ("my lord") was read instead. The Hebrew alphabet, like that of the other Semitic languages, consists of consonants only, and when during the early Middle Ages vowel points were added to the texts of Old Testament manuscripts by the copyists, they inserted the vowels for Adonai under the four consonants of YHWH, indicating that instead of *Yahweh*, the word *Adonai* was to be read aloud. The reason for this had been forgotten by modern times, and early translators of the Bible read the name of the Deity with the vowels of *Adonai*, giving the nonexistent name "Jehovah." The term is never used by anyone with the slightest knowledge of Biblical scholarship.

Yajur Veda: one of the four groups of the VEDAS, consisting of sacrificial texts.

Yakshas: in Hindu myth, the evil spirits led by RAVANA, and identical with the RAKSHAS (RAKSHASAS).

Yama: in Hindu myth, one of the ADITYAS, guardian deities of the months, and ruler over the nether world and the south.

Yami: in Hindu myth, sister and/or wife of YAMA.

Yazatas: in ancient Persian (Zoroastrian) myth, primordial deities to whom hymns in the ZEND-AVESTA are addressed.

Yen-Wang: in Chinese myth, the name of YAMA, lord of the realms of the dead in Hindu myth, However, in Chinese belief he has no power over those who by their excellence on earth pass to higher planes of existence.

Yggdrasil: in Norse myth, the giant ash tree which is the foundation of the universe. Its deepest reaches are in NIFLHEIM, and the serpent NIDHOGG continually gnaws at its roots.

Yima: in ancient Persian myth, the patriarch who was warned of the coming of the Deluge by AHURA-MAZDA and told to build a VAR, or cave in the hills, wherein he was to shelter himself and all living things. When the Flood was over, Ahura-Mazda sent a bird to Yima with the news.

Ymir: in Norse myth, the primordial giant (JOTUN), brought into life by the warm and animating beams emanating from MUSPELLSHEIM. With him was born the cow AUDHUMLA, whose milk nourished him. The evil race of the JOTUNS sprang from him. He was later slain by ODIN, and from his body the world was created and his blood drowned the frost-giants.

Yomi: the nether world in Japanese myth.

Yoni: in Hinduism the female generative organ particularly the vulva as a concrete symbol of PARVATI embodying the active, dynamic aspect (SHAKTI) of the principle of generation of SHIVA.

Z

Zagreus: in the Orphic recension of the Mysteries of DIONYSUS, Zagreus is the child of ZEUS and PERSEPH-ONE. Through the jealousy of HERA, the child Zagreus was beguiled by the TITANS, who tore him to pieces and proceeded to devour him. Zeus then appeared on the scene, and blasted the Titans with his thunderbolts. He succeeded in saving the heart of Zagreus, and gave it to SEMELE to eat, and from her and Zeus the divine child was reborn as Dionysus.

Zalmoxis: a minor divinity of the Getae, a people of Thrace near the Hellespont. He was said to have brought mystic lore regarding the immortality of the soul from Egypt and from Pythagoras, introducing this concept, together with the arts of civilization, to his people.

Zarathustra: traditional founder and prophet of Zoroastrianism, the dualistic religion of ancient Persia based upon the struggle between the good and evil principles represented by AHURA-MAZDA and AHRIMAN respectively. Despite the marvels attributed to him, it is likely that he was an historical personage, a religious leader who reorganized and reconstituted an older faith. The ZEND-AVESTA is purposed to be a collection of his writings.

Zarpanit: ancient Sumero-Babylonian goddess, consort of MARDUK, also known as BELTIA.

Zelus: personified Greek god of the zeal of battle, son of PALLAS and STYX and brother of BIA and NIKE.

Zend-Avesta: the sacred writings of the Zoroastrian religion of ancient Persia.

Zephyrus: Greek god of the welcome West Wind of spring, son of the TITAN Astraeus and EOS, and brother of BOREAS, EURUS and NOTUS. In Latin FAVONIUS.

Zethus: son of ZEUS and Aniope, and twin brother of AMPHION, whom he later helped in building the walls of Thebes.

Zeus: the head of the Olympian pantheon in Greece, father and king of gods and men. He was the youngest son of KRONOS and RHEA, and brother of POSEIDON, HADES, HESTIA, DEMETER, and HERA, the latter becoming also his wife. Kronos had swallowed his children as soon as they were born, but at the birth of Zeus, Rhea presented Kronos with a stone wrapped in swaddling clothes, which he devoured, believing it to be the child Zeus. Rhea then spirited away the infant Zeus to Crete, where she hid him in a cave on Mt. Ida or Dicte. There he was nourished by the goat (or nymph) AMALTHEIA, while the KOURETES drowned out his cries by the clashing of their swords against their shields during their armed dance. When he grew up, he took as his first consort METIS, an ancient powerful goddess, who by means of a charm had made Kronos disgorge the children whom he had swallowed. With the aid of his brother and sister deities, Zeus then overthrew Kronos and the TITANS and divided the rule of the cosmos with his brothers Poseidon and Hades, Zeus obtaining the general kingship and the specific domain of the upper air and the heavens. When Metis was pregnant by him, he swallowed her, so that she might not give birth to a son who would displace him, and in consequence ATHENA was born from his forehead. By other goddesses and mortal women Zeus became the father of many deities and heroes, their various vicissitudes usually being occasioned by the vindictive jealousy of his official wife, Hera. Zeus is usually regarded as ruler of the heavens and wielder of the thunder and lightning bolt, gatherer of clouds and bringer of the fertilizing rain. The eagle and the oak are sacred to him. The Romans equated him with their chief god JUPITER.

Zoroaster: Greek rendering of ZARATHUSTRA, which see.

Zotz, Zotzilaha: Mayan bat-god of the caves mentioned in the Central American creation legends.

Zu: in Sumero-Akkadian myth, the divine storm-bird who stole the Tablets of Destiny from ENLIL and hid them on a mountaintop. ANU ordered several gods in turn to retrieve them, but all were afraid. According to one text, MARDUK killed the Zu-bird and recovered the tablets.